Photographing Greatness

The Story of Karsh

Stories of Canada

Photographing Greatness

The Story of Karsh

by

lian goodall

Illustrations by Samantha Thompson

Napoleon

Napoleon & Company
Toronto Ontario Canada
www.napoleonandcompany.com

Le Conseil des Arts | The Canada Council
du Canada | for the Arts

Napoleon & Company acknowledges
the support of the Canada Council
for our publishing program.

Printed in Canada

11 10 09 08 07   5 4 3 2 1

Library and Archives Canada Cataloguing in Publication

Goodall, Lian
        Photographing greatness : the story of Karsh / Lian Goodall.

(Stories of Canada)
Includes bibliographical references and index.
ISBN 978-1-894917-34-6

        1. Karsh, Yousuf, 1908-2002--Juvenile literature. 2. Portrait
photographers--Canada--Biography--Juvenile literature.
3. Photographers--Canada--Biography--Juvenile literature.
I. Title. II. Series: Stories of Canada (Toronto, Ont.)
TR140.K3G66 2007   j779'.2092   C2007-903849-2

This story is for my father, Ron Goodall, a great dad for a kid who was curious about art and science.

Introduction

In your mind, how do you see the faces of your favourite people? When we think of well-known people of the twentieth century, a dramatically lit, black and white photograph by Yousuf Karsh may come to mind. He began his career in 1932, and for the next sixty years, Yousuf's portraits gave magazine, newspaper and book readers the feeling that they personally knew many important people.

The photographer's positive reflection of the world is amazing considering that as a boy he survived the murder of thousands of Armenians in Turkey. After his family escaped the country, teenaged Yousuf emigrated to Canada and worked in his uncle's photography studio. Pieces of his story are found in articles and books by Yousuf, family members and other writers. Other parts are uncovered in the letters, papers and photographs at the Library and Archives Canada. But some facts about Yousuf's flight from Turkey to Syria and his rise to fame were never recorded and remain unknown.

We do know that from boyhood on, Yousuf did his best to help his family. Once he had discovered his passion for portrait photography, he worked hard to become the best in his field, in his new country and in the world. The *International Who's Who* included the name "Yousuf Karsh" in its list of the most influential figures of the twentieth century.

BEING "KARSHED"

"I've been Karshed," said General Montgomery after he was photographed in 1943. People would understand this to mean, "I have been made immortal by the best portrait photographer of our time." Karsh photographs found their way around the world on stamps, bank notes and even potato wrappers.

Many of the others on the list—kings, queens, politicians, scientists, musicians, sports heroes and movie stars—had had their portraits made by Karsh of Ottawa. It was an incredible achievement.

Through his camera lens, Yousuf seemed able to reveal a subject's very soul. You will notice the faces are surprisingly real, but there is also mystery that will call you to look at the photographs again and again.

While Yousuf found it challenging to photograph those people who left a mark on the world, it was not only the famous that he photographed. Whether the subject was a worker in a factory or a child with muscular dystrophy, Yousuf strove to find the greatness in each person.

This photo by Karsh shows Lord Mountbatten, a British politician who is best known overseeing the division of British India into the independent states of India and Pakistan in 1947. *Maclean's* is a famous Canadian news magazine that is still published today.

YOUSUF'S PARENTS

Yousuf's parents were both Christian, but they worshipped at different churches. Yousuf's mother went to a Protestant church. Yousuf's father, Amish (or Abdel Massih), was a member of the Roman Catholic Church. The priest had not been too happy when Amish had decided to marry a non-Catholic, but Amish followed his heart. Amish Karsh and Bahia Nakash were married in 1902. Their children learned about both Catholicism and Protestantism.

First Days in Mardin

Baby Yousuf was born on December 23, 1908 at his grandmother's house in Mardin, Turkey. It was just before Christmas, a special holy time for his family, who were Christian Armenians. Yousuf was baptized into the Roman Catholic Church a few days after he was born.

Armenians were some of the first people in the world to become Christian, more than 1,700 years ago. But over the centuries, different groups ruled the area. In Turkey, where Yousuf was born, the rulers and most people had a different language, culture and religion from Armenians.

Mardin, the town where Yousuf's family lived, was in southern Turkey. Mardin had been a Christian town in the third century, but in 640, Muslim Arabs occupied the city. When Yousuf was born, the city had a dozen different ethnic groups and religions, and most people were Muslim.

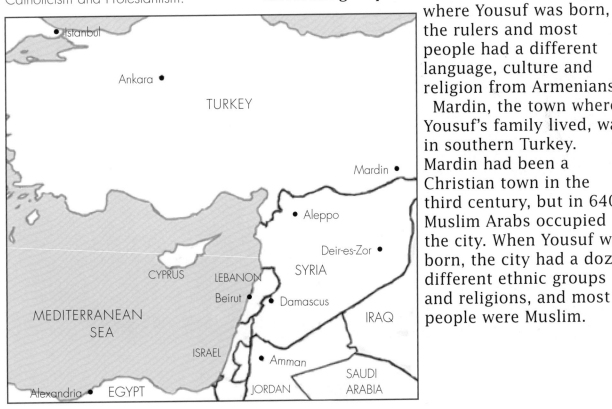

The town sat on the slope of a large plateau overlooking the plains of northern Syria. Mardin had lovely fruit trees and old stone houses. For hundreds of years, the talented townspeople had woven carpets for their homes and chipped carvings into the stone walls of the buildings to decorate the town.

Yousuf's family was artistic. His grandfather Nakash was a goldsmith and engraver. The word "nakash" meant engraver. Some of his uncles worked at artistic writing or calligraphy. Yousuf, as an adult, said that his father had imported and exported "beautiful things", furniture and handmade rugs. Yousuf fondly remembered the peace of his first years of life.

When he was five years old, Yousuf went to the Protestant mission school. Grandmother Nakash took him through the winding streets on her back. She dropped him off with some peanuts for his snack. Yousuf loved kindergarten. He had no toys at home. At school he played with wooden blocks and beads on wires. Two years later, Yousuf went to a Roman Catholic school. Yousuf's teachers thought that the smart, friendly boy might one day become a priest.

The Loss of Safety

Every child should feel safe. In 1915, Christian Armenians, even the children, were no longer safe. It seemed that the Turkish government at the beginning of the First World War wanted to destroy all Armenians in Turkey. Armenians were murdered, and thousands more died when they were deported and forced to march out of the country through desert-like areas and over mountains.

The Karsh children learned to speak Arabic so they wouldn't stand out. Even so, some children showed hatred towards them. Yousuf's marbles were stolen, and one day boys threw stones at him as he walked home from school.

At home, his mother cleaned the cut on his head as Yousuf angrily talked about his plan to throw pebbles back at the mean boys. Bahia's gentle brown eyes looked into her son's stormy, dark ones. She understood how Yousuf felt the need to protect himself, but if he threw a stone, she warned, "Be sure you miss."

FEAR

Experts think 1.5 million Armenians were murdered or died from hunger and disease between 1915 and 1922. In April 2004, the Canadian House of Commons recognized the Armenian genocide of 1915 as a "crime against humanity". Canada, France, Italy, Israel and others thought that the government in power in Turkey at that time had planned to kill all Armenians in the land.

Father's Trials

A MISSIONARY IN TURKEY

At age nine, Ada Barker (Moyer) decided to become a missionary. In 1900, when she was twenty-five, Ada left Vineland, Ontario, and joined those helping Armenian orphans in Hadjin, Turkey. In 1915, Turkey sided with Germany during the First World War, and the missionaries were ordered to leave. Back in North America, Ada helped the first orphaned Armenian boys come to Canada. Ada was the great-great-aunt of the author of this book. She lived to be 107.

Many Armenian men were taken by the army, never to return. When the army took Yousuf's father away, the family was afraid for his life. Later, one family member explained how luck and kindness saved Amish. A head soldier found out Amish was the nephew of Abdel-Ahad Karsh. Abdel-Ahad and the officer had probably worked together. They had shared bread and salt, an Islamic custom that made them like brothers. The officer spared the life of Abdel-Ahad's nephew.

Amish was not killed, but he was forced to work for the army. The story says Amish was made to appraise, or give a price, to rings, necklaces and jewels. Because the jewellery was stolen from Armenians, Amish hated this job. His blue eyes were often filled with sadness and his heart sick, but he loved his family more than anything, and he wanted to survive to see them again.

Some members of the Barker family, around 1905, probably taken in Baghdad: Thomas, Ada, Evangeline (Van), Ruth and Ted.

Death and Dreaming

ARMENIANS' WAY WITH WORDS

One Armenian saying is, "The world is but a pot and humans but spoons in it." Sharing stories and sayings helped Armenians value their place in the world, keep faith, or even laugh. Bahia read stories from the Bible to her children. Yousuf's father and brothers told the funniest and most beautiful tales. As an adult, Yousuf was known as a storyteller with many yarns to share.

Two of Yousuf's uncles, his mother's brothers, were taken to prison. Every day, young Yousuf took food to the jail for them. It was terrifying for the little boy. He bravely delivered a big package for the guards and a small package that he hoped the guards would give his uncles. Tragically, the uncles were eventually murdered.

A horrible disease swept through the town of Mardin. People were already weak with hunger, and many died from the spread of typhoid fever. One story says that Yousuf had two older brothers who died from the disease. Yousuf remembered an older sister, Josephine, who became ill and died. Bahia did not want her beloved Yousuf to catch typhus. She gave him a tin cup and told him to drink from nothing else, hoping that he would not get sick.

Bahia refused to lose her faith or lessen her kindness. She took in a girl who was blinded by the soldiers. Yousuf's mother showed the girl how to crochet and other ways to use her hands. Bahia gave her some of the little bit of black bread they had. She shared their water, even though Bahia had to walk very far to fetch it in a bucket.

Life seemed impossibly difficult, but even during bad times, children still hope and dream. The children of Mardin dreamed of better days and safer places. They had

8

hundreds of years of powerful stories to feed the journeys of their minds. Yousuf had a young girl cousin who would tell stories like the ones of a *Thousand and One Nights.* On hot evenings, they lay on their mattresses on the roof, watching the stars come out. The words of the tales let them escape to splendid places; the descriptions of beauty and bravery inspired the children.

Pile of Bones

NEVER FORGETTING SOLDIER GREEN

Yousuf did not want to remember hatred all his life. But some things stay deep in people's minds. When he was grown up, his sister-in-law Barbara visited, wearing a green dress. Yousuf seemed upset and left the room for a while. It was explained to Barbara that the green colour of her dress made Yousuf remember the soldiers' green uniforms.

At last, the Karsh family was allowed to leave Turkey. With some other survivors, they crossed the desert. Exactly who left and when they went is hard to know. Written records do not exist, and family members tell the story differently. Amish, Bahia, Yousuf and his brother Malak (born in 1915), and probably Jamil (born in 1920), made the trip to Syria. On foot and by mule, it took three weeks through terrain that was often dry, or rugged and steep.

At one stop, Yousuf saw a pile of human bones —most likely the remains of Armenians who would never finish their journey. Yousuf began to draw the skulls, to record the terrible things that he never wanted to see again. When someone spotted him, frightened Yousuf threw the paper into the river, but it floated among the bodies.

The men in charge did not want pictures of their diabolical deeds to leave the country. They angrily called Yousuf's father. Amish paid them some of the Karshes' last coins, and the family escaped.

Starting Again

Armenian refugees in 1915 await their fate in a refugee camp.

Thousands of Armenians stayed in tents in the city of Aleppo, in Syria. The Karshes and other refugees had little but their faith, determination and each other.

The family needed money for food and to send Yousuf to a Catholic school. Though Amish could not read, he felt that education would give his sons a better chance in life. Amish knit socks by machine, working until his fingers could no longer move.

Relatives told the family that life might be better if they moved to another city in Syria, Deir-es-Zor. Once there, the Karshes found shelter in a church where the courtyard had been turned into four rooms. One family lived in each room.

Amish tried to find work. Bahia also looked for ways to improve her sons' futures. Her younger brother George lived in Canada. Bahia urged George to take her eldest son, whom he had never met. "He is quite bright," she wrote. "Yousuf would make a good doctor."

COULD YOU START AGAIN?

Starting life in a new country might be an adventure. But times can be tough if you are arriving with no money at a place where you have no family, and you don't speak the language. Your parents' education and job training might not be recognized. If your mother was a doctor at home, she might not be able to be a doctor in the new country.

Saying Goodbye

ONE OF THE FIRST IN CANADA

Yousuf's great-uncle was one of the first Armenians to come to Canada. Aziz Sarafian started a clothing store not too far from Quebec City in the Thetford Mines area of Quebec in the early 1900s. He saved money so that he could help others come to safety in Canada. Aziz Sarafian changed his last name to Setlakwé, which means six brothers, to honour his five brothers who were killed in Turkey.

When he learned he was to go to Canada, Yousuf felt both excited and worried. He had some family in Canada, but how could he be so far from his beloved mother, father, and his brothers, Malak and Jamil?

Yousuf had to return to Aleppo by himself and stay with an aunt. He had to wait while his papers were prepared and while he learned some French and English. The Karsh family cried bitterly as they said goodbye at the bus station. The fourteen-year-old boy made the ten-hour journey alone, with only his bedding and a heavy heart.

After two months in Aleppo, Yousuf took the train to Beirut, Lebanon. He stayed with some distant cousins until they all left for Canada.

Yousuf often felt sad. The teenager did not feel close to the people he was with. He missed his family. Yousuf had many feelings churning inside him: fear and loneliness, but also hope.

Aleppo is one of the oldest inhabited cities in the world.

Ocean Voyage

The ship the *Canada* sailed in the late fall of 1923. For the first few days, many passengers were seasick. Soon, however, the children were out exploring and playing ball or other games. Some passengers played cards, while others chatted. After Yousuf settled into life in second class, the nearly month-long journey seemed to pass slowly. On deck, he turned his eyes towards the cold, grey skies in the east, the direction of his past. Then he gazed wonderingly towards the west, the direction which held his future.

The week before they reached Canada, everyone became excited. Yousuf passed his fifteenth birthday on the ship, with more questions wriggling in his head. When would he see his parents and his brothers again? What job could a teenaged immigrant find to help him live and to help his family? What was Canada like? What was Uncle George like?

THE GEORGETOWN BOYS

Before the 1930s, thousands of children under age of sixteen were brought to North America. They often worked on farms or as servants. In 1923, some Armenian boys came to Canada through the Armenian Relief Society. They stayed on a farm near Georgetown, Ontario, and were called the "Georgetown Boys". They learned English and farming before going to help farm families. Some of the Georgetown Boys thought they would find the streets in Canada paved with gold.

Armenian boys in Canada

13

Arrival in Canada

ARRIVING IN HALIFAX

Pier 2 saw more than 27 million people arrive from other countries between 1911 and 1928. After 1928, immigrants arrived at Pier 21. In 1999, Pier 21 became a museum and national historic site that celebrates the history of those immigrants who came to Canada through the port of Halifax.

The immigration sheds at Pier 2, where new Canadians came ashore

The passengers of the *Canada* filed off the ship at the port of Halifax, Nova Scotia. Uncle George had a photograph of Yousuf in his hand. As soon as George spotted his nephew, he joyfully greeted him in Arabic. Yousuf felt happy to hear a language he understood among the foreign sounds swirling around him.

Yousuf and his uncle waited in a big hall at Pier 2. Immigration officers checked Yousuf's papers once, twice and then again. Night came, and still they waited. Nephew and uncle lay on bunks in a huge room, worrying and trying to sleep. Yousuf had almost no baggage or money. George Nakash had promised the Canadian government he would support his nephew. Would that be enough?

In the morning, an official filled in form 30A, "Declaration of Passenger to Canada". "Youssef Kerch", he wrote. Perhaps Yousuf did not speak enough English to fix the spelling mistake in his last name. Or perhaps he did not dare. The form said he was age fifteen, that he had arrived January 1, 1924, at Halifax, travelling on a Syrian passport. It stated that he had fifteen dollars and he was coming to Canada "to join his uncle". The new immigrant signed his name on the document as "Youseph Karsh".

Finally, Uncle George and Yousuf could leave. A sleigh-taxi took them up Cornwallis Street towards the train station. The bells on the horses seemed to jingle with the excitement of a new year and a new beginning. Yousuf marvelled at all he heard and saw on the Halifax streets. And snow! Everything was new and special to the teenager's wondering eyes.

The train chugged through the provinces of Nova Scotia and New Brunswick, gobbling up hour after hour of majestic white countryside. But the beautiful snow was also a powerful force. Yousuf remembered later that the train became stuck in deep snow for so long that he felt something familiar—hunger. Soon the train was freed and moving them towards Yousuf's new home in Sherbrooke, Quebec.

Uncle George's Photography

GEORGE NAKASH

By 1934, George had moved to Montreal, Quebec. George took photographs there until just a few years before he died in 1976. He made lovely portraits of children and some famous people such as the mayor of Montreal. George was one of the first photographers to make portraits that included the sitter's hands, something Yousuf would also do. Yousuf said his uncle taught him the basics of photography and how to be "gracious" with people.

George Nakash (or Nakashian) was born in 1892. He was one of Bahia's seven siblings. When he was a teenager, George's uncles helped him leave Turkey. Three of his brothers, Charo, Salim and Chafik, would not be so lucky and were murdered.

George rode a horse to Syria and eventually made his way to the city of Beirut in the country of Lebanon. Around 1910, a cousin gave him a sales job in a department store.

The store had a photography studio. George loved photographs. When he was ten years old, he had first seen what he called "the magic of photography". The camera belonged to a friend of his father's, who had brought it from New York.

At the store, George hung around the studio until he was told he could be a helper there. He said it was "one of the happiest moments" of his life.

One day, while the photographers were out at lunch, an important French diplomat came in. "Who's going to photograph him?" George asked.

George Nakash

"You!" a store worker replied.

When the portraits pleased the diplomat, George knew he wanted to become a photographer.

He left Beirut and moved to New York with the help of his uncle Aziz Setlakwé. George worked in a photography studio, but he became very ill. Uncle Aziz came from Canada to fetch his sick nephew.

Aziz always wanted to help others. In February 1914, he was glad to bring his nephew to his home in the province of Quebec and to give him a job in his store.

Soon, George was better and travelling around the countryside taking photographs. As he grew more skilled, he found that taking pictures of people, or portraits, was a good trade. Around 1918 he opened a studio in Sherbrooke. By 1919, he was able to take his turn helping his family. He went to collect his sister Nazlia from Egypt. Several years later, he had enough business to need a helper. Bahia's son, Yousuf, would be that helper.

Yousuf with his Aunt Nazlia, Aunt Lucia and her young son, Camil Darac.

School the First Winter

LEARNING ENGLISH

Yousuf went to mass in the Roman Catholic Church (the church his father had attended), but he also went to a Protestant Sunday School (his mother's church). A Protestant minister was one of the friendly people who gave Yousuf English lessons. For many years, he worked hard to perfect his English skills.

Even though it was the middle of the school year, Uncle George wanted his nephew to start school, but Yousuf did not have as much schooling as many Canadians his age. Another challenge was language. He spoke languages such as Arabic very well, but only some French and a tiny bit of English. Uncle George put Yousuf in an English school to improve his English. At Cambridge School, he was placed in the highest grade for French classes, but for some subjects he was in a lower grade, sometimes in Grade Four.

The first day, Yousuf didn't understand much of what the teacher, Mrs. Hatch, said. As she introduced him, he stood in front of the class under the gaze of many curious eyes. He smiled and bowed, for he always tried to be as polite as possible.

When he took his seat, one girl, Margaret Bradley, tried to make friends right away. She scribbled notes to him in English. He wrote back in

Cambridge School

his language. It didn't matter what the notes said, it was the wish to start communicating that was important.

At recess, away from the teachers, Yousuf may have fretted because of his memories of cruel school-mates in Mardin. But when he won a marble, the players in Sherbrooke said, "Keep it." Yousuf felt lucky. He would tell the story over and over again for years to come. It was then that he knew he loved Canada.

That winter, Yousuf had a lot of fun getting to know Sherbrooke.

He also began snowshoeing. The first time he tried it was when he entered a contest—and he won. On bright moonlit nights, he enjoyed tramping over the snow on snowshoes with Uncle George, who was taking photographs.

Work With Uncle George

TYPES OF PHOTOGRAPHY

Some photographers love the countryside, and they become landscape photographers. Others like news events, and they work as photojournalists. Uncle George was fascinated with the "moods and expressions" of people, so he became a portrait photographer.

An early darkroom

When summer came, Yousuf had more time to help his uncle. Sometimes in the studio, Yousuf felt embarrassed because his English was still poor. He loved jokes, but they were hard to understand in his newest language. One client, who was a member of parliament, laughed about his own looks.

"I'm afraid I'll break your camera," the man joked.

"Don't worry, we have another one," Yousuf replied seriously.

After the portraits were taken, Yousuf and his uncle worked in the dark room. It might seem as if photographs appear by magic, but he was learning that the hard work of the photographer and his or her assistant controlled that "magic". He stood for long hours, helping his uncle process the negatives, then using them to make prints. Yousuf mixed the chemicals for the solutions that both developed the negatives and made the prints on light-sensitive paper. He had to pay attention to the time of each chemical bath and many other details.

After Yousuf had learned the basics, he wanted to improve quickly. Prints look best if there is a lot of contrast between the lights and the darks and there are many tones of grey in between. It was hard to get things perfect, and the young assistant often became discouraged.

Uncle George knew his nephew was upset. He wondered if Yousuf really wanted to be a photographer. He suggested that Yousuf think about his future then come talk to him.

People had thought Yousuf would become a priest or a doctor, but it would be hard to catch up with the schooling these professions needed, and he felt he was done with his formal education. He could learn by watching and helping others, and perhaps be paid a little. That seemed the fastest way to soon be able to send money to his family.

For many reasons, being a photographer seemed like a good job to Yousuf. Above all, photography was beginning to interest him deeply.

A photo by George Nakash. Nakash had a gift for making portraits of people of all ages.

THE BROWNIE CAMERA
AND KODAK

The Brownies were characters in children's books by Canadian Palmer Cox. In 1900, the Kodak Company made the Brownie camera for young people. It only cost a dollar. George Eastman, who founded Kodak, had changed photography with the first easy-to-use cameras in 1888. Before that, people had to develop the glass plate negatives then make the prints themselves. But Kodak had people mail them the entire camera, with the roll of exposed film still in it. Kodak developed the film and returned the camera and completed prints. Much easier!

Yousuf's prize-winning photo →

First Prize

After only two weeks, Yousuf told his uncle that he wanted to become a photographer.

"Why?" asked Uncle George.

"Because I love it," Yousuf answered shyly, his dark eyes gleaming.

With his mind made up, Yousuf worked even harder. George later said, "I have never seen anyone with such dedication."

The teen began experimenting with a Brownie camera which George had given him. Yousuf gave one of his photographs to a friend. It was a print of a landscape with

some children playing. In secret, the friend entered it in a contest with the T. Eaton Company in 1926. Yousuf was surprised when he won the fifty dollar first prize!

He kept only ten dollars and proudly mailed the rest to his parents. He felt as if he were sending "four million" dollars.

Yousuf said later, "I walked straight for weeks on end." Helping his family was one of the most important things he felt he could do.

22

An Educational Adventure in Boston

Garo in his artist's smock poses for young Karsh

JOHN GARO

Most of Garo's immediate family died in Harpoot, Turkey. Other members of Garo's family brought him to the Boston area when he was fourteen years old. After apprenticing with a photographer, Garo opened his own studio in 1902 at age twenty-seven. Garo's photographs had a special way of showing the character of the sitter, as Yousuf's would.

After Garo died in 1939, one person close to Yousuf said, "It is because of Garo that there is a Karsh."

Today, students can choose from many photography courses. In the 1920s, photographers gained skills by working as apprentices with someone who was an expert. To help Yousuf learn more, George contacted his friend, John Garo. Mr. Garo had judged a contest that George had entered in 1921. This man was an important photographer in the Boston area of Massachusetts, in the United States, and a fellow Armenian. Mr. Garo, or Garoian, had many friends who called him simply "Garo". George arranged an apprenticeship with Garo, and Yousuf had to move, yet again, to another country. At twenty years old, he was embarking on another new adventure.

He thought he would be in Boston for only six months. However, Yousuf would stay with Garo for three years, from 1928 to 1931. he found Garo to be a kind man and an excellent teacher.

Seeing

LIGHT

"Photography" comes from the Greek words that mean "to draw with light". In a camera, light enters through an opening, or aperture, past the open shutter and into a lightproof box. Here an image is recorded on a special surface that photographers prepared in the dark before putting it in the back of the box. The first cameras of 1839 could take half an hour to collect light from a scene and record the image. Now images are recorded on a microchip rather than metal (the first material used), glass or film. But light remains key.

Garo usually wore an artist's smock because he loved painting with oils. As a painter and a photographer, Garo challenged his apprentice to "see" or envision and also feel a picture before taking a photograph.

One winter day, he told Yousuf to look out the window. "What do you see?" Garo asked.

Yousuf reported the patterns he detected in the snow. Then Garo described the patterns he saw. The master's vision was very different from the young man's. Yousuf didn't understand. "I have brown eyes like yours!" he exclaimed.

"Your eyes," Garo said, "should not see exactly the way mine do. If you copy me, you will have learned nothing."

The apprentice gained precious knowledge at Garo's studio and the confidence to develop his own style. Yousuf would also say, "one must learn to see with one's mind's eye, for the heart and the mind are the true lens of the camera."

lens mirror screen film

object

shutter

film image

Beyond the Camera

The Museum of Fine Arts, Boston

ART IN BOSTON

In 1907, the Museum of Fine Arts, Boston was housed in an elegant stone building with huge 152-metre (500-feet) high columns beside the doors. Yousuf returned there to hold his first major American show in 1968.

Although modern photography began in 1839, in the 1920s photography was still thought of as so new that many people were only just beginning to think of it as art. For centuries, painters had already been perfecting lighting and composition (or how to arrange a picture). To prepare Yousuf to be a camera artist, Garo insisted he find out about all kinds of art.

In the evenings, the hard-working student took art classes. He would never be a painter like Garo, or the best in the class, but Yousuf enjoyed helping the teacher. To prepare for the class, models or objects were posed against background material. He draped, or arranged, the folds of the fabric. As he learned to compose a picture, Yousuf noted the effects of the light and shadow, exactly what a photographer needs to know.

To learn more about paintings, he visited the Museum of Fine Arts, Boston. Once he entered the stately museum, Yousuf dreamed while gazing at the works of famous artists such as El Greco, Rembrandt and Goya. In 1928, he might even have viewed an exhibit of one of the most important photographers of the day, Alfred Stieglitz. Yousuf felt happy and at home in the museum.

Garo also sent Yousuf down the street from the studio to look at art books in the Boston Public Library. Statues of some of the world's greatest thinkers decorated the wide stairs leading to the library building. The words "Free to All" were carved in the stone above the doors. Yousuf was excited to be entering a palace of knowledge, a place for everyone. The library would be another of his special "homes" in Boston.

A photo of Yousuf taken by Garo in 1933

Learning About People

CHARMING YOUSUF

Yousuf later told young people to learn about many things, not just about photography. His interests were broadened by meeting Garo's talented friends. Garo's guests were impressed by his young apprentice with the shy eyes and warm smile. As he grew older, Yousuf grew less shy, but he stayed polite and kind. His charming ways helped his clients relax in front of the camera.

A man is arrested for possession of alcohol, which at the time was illegal in the U.S. and parts of Canada.

Garo worked mostly with sunlight that came through the large skylights into the third-floor studio. When it was rainy or dark, Garo stopped work. That was when his special friends came to visit.

Musicians, writers and other clever people gathered to enjoy Garo's company and perhaps a drink. During the time from 1922 to 1930, known as Prohibition, alcohol was outlawed in the United States (and in parts of Canada). Many of Garo's friends thought this was too strict. Alcohol came to the studio delivered in paint tins.

Some visitors tried a drink Armenians knew as "raki" or "lion's milk". Other drinks had code names after the toxic chemicals used in the photography fixing process. Using these secret names, Garo might tell his young assistant to bring a guest a drink of "hypo". In reality, hyposulphite of soda was a very poisonous chemical that was definitely not a drink. Of course, the guest was not given "hypo", but an alcoholic drink.

As rain dribbled down the glass skylight, the visitors sat around a tiger-skin rug near a gigantic fireplace. Garo might sing opera in his strong voice, with his nephew accompanying him on the piano. Or a visiting singer might perform. Yousuf loved the sound of rich voices.

The young apprentice found the music, the conversation, and the feeling in the studio to be inspiring. Now in his twenties, he knew exactly what he would do. Like his uncle and his master, Yousuf would become a portrait photographer. He would try hard to reveal the very soul of a person through the camera.

At the Boylston Street studio, Yousuf also started to think it would be challenging to photograph interesting and gifted people. "Even as a young man," he said later in life, "I was aware that these glorious afternoons and evenings in Garo's salon were my university. There I set my heart on photographing those men and women who leave their mark on their world."

Immigration Worries

PORTRAIT PHOTOGRAPHY

When the first practical cameras appeared in 1839, people were excited to have what they considered to be a real likeness of themselves. Photographs could be made more quickly and cheaply than paintings. The detailed daguerreotypes of the 1840s and 1850s quickly became very popular; people loved giving *cartes de visite* with their photographs on them as gifts to friends. Gradually, portrait photographs became used for passports and fashion advertising. By the 1920s, photographers used a soft, dreamy or "Pictoralist" look.

A *carte de visite* photo from the nineteenth century. The images on these cards could often be quite creative.

Ralph Sadler, a man who worked for the *Boston Transcript* newspaper, was one visitor to the studio. He later wrote Yousuf a letter that said he loved the glow of Mr. Garo's "friendship and wisdom and great good humour". One dark, rainy day Ralph arrived to find the studio "for the first and only time— as depressing indoors as out. No singing. No excitement." When he asked what was wrong, he was told, "Yousuf's immigration permit has run out," or was about to. Ralph was able to save the day. He had a highly-placed friend who fixed the problem through his government connections. "Within a day or so, we learned that Yousuf's indefinite residence on this side of the ocean was assured."

People who immigrate to a new country must keep their visas, permits and work papers in order. Yousuf must have felt lucky not to have these worries any more.

To the Capital of Canada

PHOTOGRAPHERS YOUSUF ADMIRED

Dorothy Wilding (1893–1976) and Edward Steichen (1879–1973), were two photographers whose fashion photographs Karsh kept in his scrapbook. Rather than the soft style of the 1920s, these two photographers of the 1930s were moving towards an edgy, almost art deco style that Yousuf would try. When Yousuf was just starting out, he met Steichen. Yousuf photographed the man whose work he admired in 1944, again in 1967, and in 1970 when Steichen was in his nineties.

ART DECO

Early photographers tried to make their photographs look almost like romantic oil paintings. When Yousuf started out, daring young photographers were using a new style known as Art Deco. The fuzzy, soft-looking pictures were replaced by sharply focused ones with bold shapes created by light and shadow.

After three years, Yousuf Karsh returned to Sherbrooke, Quebec. His Uncle George had married and was starting a family. In 1932, at age twenty-four, Yousuf knew it was time to go out on his own.

Which city, he wondered, would be the best for his future portrait studio: London, England; New York, U.S.A.; or Ottawa, Ontario, Canada? Ottawa won. Yousuf knew that many important people (and hopefully possible clients) visited the capital of his adopted country.

Yousuf found work as an assistant with a photographer, Mr. John Powis. Mr. Powis had made portraits of important people in Ottawa, such as the mayor and the Governor General of Canada. His studio was in the Hardy Arcade at 130 Sparks Street, one block from the parliament buildings.

With his two suitcases, Yousuf checked into a room at the Y.M.C.A. There he met John Henderson from Ireland. Neither newcomer could wait to explore. Yousuf took John to a beautiful natural area, the Gatineau Hills in nearby Quebec. Years later, John wrote to him, "I shall always remember you as the one who opened my eyes to the wonder and beauty of Nature on a Canadian hillside long ago."

Yousuf often took a camera even on picnics and spent time practising his technique everywhere he went. He also learned about photography by keeping scrapbooks of clippings from magazines. By studying the modern fashion photographs of Dorothy Wilding and Edward Steichen, he collected ideas about how to portray people.

OPEN DOOR

The Karsh studio welcomed many young photographers through its doors from the first days it opened to the day it closed. Yousuf always tried to find time to look at their work and give helpful comments. Once, when he was talking to a budding teen photographer in an airport, Yousuf postponed his flight. The reason? He was busy talking to his "young colleague".

The young man wanted to quit school to become a photographer, but Yousuf convinced him to finish school first and learn more about art and life in order to become a better photographer. The fifteen-year-old followed the advice and later became a photographer.

His Own Studio

When Mr. Powis moved from Sparks Street, Yousuf borrowed money from a relative and took over the studio.

His business was launched—Karsh of Ottawa.

He was determined to see it succeed, even though inside his studio, the "furniture" was mostly wooden crates covered with rough fabric. The young businessman sometimes had to borrow back some of the money he paid his secretary. He could not send a lot to his family, or repay much of his debt, but he would work hard to change this.

In 1932, there were already twelve photographers in Ottawa. To get ahead, Yousuf sent out letters inviting people to come to the studio and advertised his "Modern Photographic Studio" in the newspaper. The 1930s was a period of economic hard times known as the Depression. People had no money for extras, but the studio's clever ads informed them that "good photographs are not expensive."

One of Yousuf's 1934 theatre photos labelled "Ottawa Ladies College: Miss Currie's Group"

First Clients

CREATIVE, FLEXIBLE, PREPARED AND FAST

No matter how many photographs Yousuf took of debutantes or brides, he needed to make each one look different. Photographers have to be creative, but also flexible. Actors or politicians often had little time to give to him. "Five minutes!" were words that he didn't like to hear. To work quickly, he prepared for every sitting in advance. He found out about the sitter, came up with some ideas for poses, and perhaps even practised the lighting ahead of time.

Debutantes often posed for a special photograph, such as this one by an unknown photographer.

Beside the staircase leading up to the studio was a showcase where people could view Yousuf's latest portraits. Passers-by admired the smiling faces of the babies, students, mothers, businessmen and diplomats made for special occasions, passports and press releases.

Many of the studio's first clients were brides and young women called debutantes. Debutantes had their portraits taken when they were "presented" or introduced to the Governor General at a fancy ball. The pages of popular magazines were crowded with hundreds of photographs of debutantes in their lovely dresses. But even early in his career, Yousuf's unique way of lighting and composing the pictures made his photographs stand out from the others. Perhaps all the draping in art class helped him with the ladies' long gowns.

The studio advertisement said Yousuf could "reveal the charm and beauty of the subject." Happy clients and magazine editors were finding that this claim was true.

At the Theatre

YOUSUF, THE WOLF, AND THEATRE

To raise money for music in Ottawa in 1957, Yousuf starred in *Peter and the Wolf*. Peter-Yousuf skipped merrily across the stage in funny short pants and striped socks.

When the Ottawa Little Theatre burned down in 1970, Yousuf gave his support for a new theatre. He said that he hoped not only French and English, but also the languages of ethnic groups would be spoken there "with the warm Canadian spirit".

A friend invited Yousuf to see a play one evening. Yousuf loved stories and plays. Make-believe had been one way to escape the horrible reality of his childhood. At the theatre in Ottawa, the audience felt an excited shiver when the lights went down and the stage flooded with magic.

The young men liked the play and went backstage to meet the actors. Yousuf wanted to know more about one actor, a woman with dancing blue eyes and wavy brown hair— Solange Gauthier.

One of the first photographs Yousuf printed at his new studio was of Solange wearing a costume. He took photographs of Solange, other actors and the officials of the Dominion Drama Festival in April 1933. Photograph Number One recorded in the Karsh Studio books is Nancy Barrow in the play *Will Shakespeare.* Photograph Number Seven is Solange Gauthier in *La Belle Huengua.*

This 1934 picture of Solange in costume for a play is an early photograph from the Karsh studio.

A WEDDING

Yousuf and Solange were married on April 27, 1939. A letter from Syria said that the family had cried tears of joy upon hearing the news. The couple couldn't go to meet the family, but they did go to Boston to meet the man who was like a father to Yousuf. Solange was nervous, but Garo quickly gave her a big hug.

Yousuf took a photograph of the happy occasion of Solange meeting Garo in his Boston studio.

Sparkling Solange

Solange was born on July 14, 1901, in Tours, France. When she was ten, the Gauthier family moved to Montreal, Quebec. Mr. Gauthier died soon after, and Mrs. Gauthier had to find work. She became a teacher in Ottawa and moved there with her children, Henri and Solange. When Solange grew up, she was unhappily married for a short time and worked as a translator. She spent her free time acting at the theatre and was one of the first people in the Ottawa Drama League to play roles in both of Canada's official languages, French and English.

By 1932, when Solange met Yousuf, she spoke English well but with a charming French accent. Her heart went out to the man she called a "strange and gentle foreigner". Some years later, she told a women's group what she had liked best about him. She noted his voice, his polite manners and his "sensitive and beautiful hands". But the first thing she had noticed was his great smile. "When Karsh smiles at you," she sighed, "you will think he is the most charming man you have ever met."

Right away, Solange sensed that Yousuf would go far. "From the beginning," she insisted, "I had the greatest faith in him."

CAMERAS

To make his famous big, detailed photographs, Yousuf used large-format cameras that stood on tripods to keep them steady. A specially made glass, or lens, focused the light from the object being photographed. The lens directed the rays of light through the aperture, or opening, and the opened shutter onto the negative at the back of the camera. A cloth covered the back of the camera to keep unwanted light from entering the viewfinder. Always original, Yousuf popped under a colourful, almost magical-looking velvet cloth to check the viewfinder. Yousuf had his cameras painted almost white, as he felt black looked sad.

Under the Lights

The theatre was very important to Yousuf's career. Here he met people who changed his life. The theatre also helped publicize his work. Yousuf became the official photographer of the Dominion Drama Festival. Some Karsh of Ottawa photographs were published in the popular magazines *Mayfair* and *Saturday Night* in 1933.

The theatre also gave him ideas for photography. The lighting that created the fantasy world on stage inspired the young photographer to improve his own lighting technique.

Garo's best work was done with natural light, but the artificial lights in the theatre thrilled Yousuf. The young photographer loved how shadows added drama and how special lights created a soft mood. Unlike the sun, they could be turned on, played with and moved. He was enraptured by the way the lights were used and excited about the possibilities they presented to his photography.

These actors in the Dominion Drama League Festival play "Submerged" are on a stage that represents a submarine in this 1934 photograph by Karsh.

A Mistake with the Governor General

After several attempts, Karsh was able to make a grand photograph of Governor General Bessborough and Lady Bessborough.

One of Yousuf's new theatre friends was the son of the governor general of Canada. A photograph Yousuf took of his friend pleased the young man's important parents. Governor General Bessborough and his wife agreed to come to the Karsh studio to have their portraits made.

The novice photographer couldn't sleep the night before these grand clients came to the studio. By the time Lord and Lady Bessborough arrived, Yousuf was so jittery that he could hardly even speak. He wanted to tell Lord Bessborough to wait while he took his wife's photograph, but Yousuf's excited tongue mixed up the words. "Lord Bessborough," he said, "you may recline with my secretary."

He had not meant to tell Lord Bessborough to lie down. Yousuf had wanted to suggest that he "retire" or go to the reception area with the secretary. The young photographer felt terrible about the mistake and grew more stressed. The portraits turned out very badly.

IMPORTANT LETTERS

When Yousuf sent letters to people inviting them to have their portraits made, he showed the governor general's endorsement right on his studio's letter paper.

Letters were an important way to communicate. Letters to Syria kept Yousuf in touch with the family, and he would also send money to help his brothers with their schooling. Letters back gave news of the family and told all about his youngest brother, Salim, who was born in 1925, after Yousuf had left for Canada.

Luckily, the Bessboroughs were willing to be photographed again. This time the photographs turned out very well. They were printed on the cover of an international journal, *The London Illustrated News,* and in other magazines. Yousuf felt great. This was one of his first breaks in the world of international portrait photography.

After this, Yousuf wrote letters asking to be the official photographer for the governor general. He gave lots of reasons. He had assisted John Powis, who had photographed the governor general before Yousuf had taken over the studio. He also pointed out that he was the official photographer of the Dominion Drama Festival, and that the governor general was the patron, or special friend, of this festival. For almost a year, Yousuf sent letters, determined to succeed.

In April 1935, an envelope arrived. The letter inside informed Yousuf that he could use these words in connection with his business:

By Appointment to
Their Excellencies
the Governor General and
the Countess of Bessborough

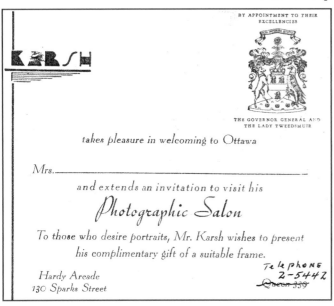

Growing Buzz

CLUES IN PHOTOGRAPHS

We can find out more about the lives of the people in Yousuf's photographs from the clothes he had the subjects wear and the objects he includes. When Yousuf placed a pen in the photograph with Margaret Atwood, people could guess that she is an author. And, even though someone may not recognize dancer Karen Kain, it's easy to guess that she is a ballerina by looking at Yousuf's photograph of her elegantly posed in a tutu.

Canadians were talking about Yousuf's one-man show at the Château Laurier hotel in Ottawa and Simpson's Gallery in Toronto. They admired photographs of Solange posing as an old lady, a dance teacher and a refugee. They marvelled at an experimental photograph of a glass bottle, which seemed to contain dancers.

People saw Karsh's work in popular magazines and read newspaper stories about the prizes he won. In 1937, one photograph made a young Ottawa girl the winner of a "Beautiful Child Contest" from out of 90,000 entries.

Karsh of Ottawa photographs began to appear at exhibits in cities around the world: Baltimore, U.S.A., London, England, and Lucknow, India. Visitors gazed at the calm eyes of the man known as Grey Owl. Yousuf was earning praise as a "modern" photographer with a clear and focused style. The growing buzz would reach the ears of the prime minister of Canada.

Karsh told environmentalist Grey Owl (Archibald Belany) that he thought this photograph showed his "courage, determination and frankness".

The Laughing
American President

THE SMILING PRIME MINISTER

In 1940, Yousuf photographed Prime Minister King smiling with his dog, Pat. King almost never smiled in photographs. From 1939 to 1945, he did not want people to think he was laughing while Canada was at war. King also had a lot on his mind. Once, King wrote in his diary that Yousuf asked Solange to talk him "out of the heavy depressed feeling which I had."

Yousuf's 1940 photo of the prime minister with his dog Pat

Yousuf was not only a good photographer, he was smart. He used one link to make others that helped his career grow. In Canada, the governor general is the head of state. The prime minister is the head of government. Yousuf had an idea for the prime minister of the time, William Lyon Mackenzie King. Yousuf suggested, as the official photographer of the governor general, he should also take photographs for the government.

The prime minister agreed to be photographed with visiting diplomats. In 1936, Yousuf was in Quebec City, when the American president met with Canada's prime minister and the new governor general. But many photographers were fluttering around outside the hotel. Yousuf fretted he would never get a shot of President Franklin D. Roosevelt and the others. A friend of Yousuf's worked for the governor general, Lord Tweedsmuir. The friend told him to stick around until the other photographers had left.

As promised, things quieted down. The governor general, the prime minister, the president and his son, came back outside. They didn't mind posing again, but Yousuf wasn't happy. He felt that they looked stiff. He pretended to take the picture then looked like he was packing up. The men relaxed, thinking

42

Prime Minister King wrote about this photograph in his diary in 1943. He thought it was "significant" that he was shown with American President Franklin D. Roosevelt under a painting of Queen Victoria.

the session was over. Lord Tweedsmuir started to tell a funny story. President Roosevelt laughed. This was when the clever photographer took the real picture.

People in public office, even the prime minister, needed fresh photographs for the press. After the Quebec visit, Prime Minister King began to use Yousuf's services more and more. Sometimes he came to the Sparks Street studio. Other times Yousuf visited Mr. King's Ottawa home or his estate in the Gatineau Hills of Quebec.

As the two got to know each other, Prime Minister King helped Yousuf in many ways. In fact, King would arrange for Karsh to take the photograph that would be the most important one of his career.

A self-portrait showing Karsh with one of his large-format cameras that were painted a light colour

Two Brothers
in Canada

MALAK'S CAMERA

Before Malak came to Canada, Yousuf sent him a camera. Yousuf longed to see his mother cooking and his father taking a walk. He told his brother such photographs would "make me feel that I am among you." Sometimes Yousuf was very lonely without his loving family.

Yousuf was getting busy. He hoped his brother Malak could come from Syria and be his assistant. Yousuf wanted to help his brother immigrate as his uncle had helped him, and as his great-uncle had helped others. But immigrating to Canada was not always easy. One immigration official even questioned the fact that Yousuf had a brother.

He did not give up, and finally, on October 3, 1937, Yousuf and Malak joyfully embraced in Canada. The two brothers had been fourteen and eight years old the last time they had seen each other. Now they were grown men.

Yousuf couldn't wait to show Malak the nearby Gatineau Hills. Malak looked at the carpet of fiery fall colours and fell in love with the land. Later, he decided to become a landscape photographer.

There was a lot to learn before Malak would become an independent photographer. He began helping everywhere: developing, retouching negatives and making prints. Near the

The Gatineau hills

The famous Karsh brothers,
Yousuf and Malak

Christmas gift-giving season, work went from seven in the morning to late at night. It was tiring, but by February, Malak wrote to Uncle George that he loved the job. "The more I see of photography, the wider the ocean grows in front of my eyes," he said. "I am not afraid of this ocean, as I will work very hard to be able to float to the surface."

Yousuf helped Malak go to New York to study photography. By 1939, he had his first photograph in a magazine. He signed his work with only his first name, "Malak", so as not to be confused with Yousuf, who signed his photographs "Karsh of Ottawa". By 1941, Malak had opened his own studio in Ottawa with his big brother's support.

Brother Jamil wrote to Yousuf that he had been sad when Malak had left, but he knew this was a step "on the way for the realization of our dreams!" The family longed to be reunited. With two Karsh brothers in Canada, they could better prepare for that long-awaited day.

Malak's Great Spirit

MALAK AND TULIPS

Malak is famous for his photographs of tulips, and for helping to start Ottawa's Tulip Festival in 1953. The Tulip Festival honours the tulips given to Canada by the Dutch people and their Princess Juliana to thank Canada for its help and for giving shelter to the royal family during the Second World War. This colourful May celebration was one of the ideas Malak had while recovering from TB.

ON THE MONEY

Malak's most admired photograph may be one of a boat on the Ottawa River towing logs past the parliament buildings. The photograph was featured on Canadian one dollar bills printed from 1973 to 1987. A portrait of Queen Elizabeth, based on his brother Yousuf's photograph, had appeared on the 1954 issue of the dollar bill.

The beautiful, clever young woman Yousuf and Solange hired to be Malak's secretary at his new studio soon became Malak's wife. Barbara Holmes and Malak had a good life together and four children, but Malak's career was put on hold by illness a few times. Not long after he opened his studio, doctors told him he had tuberculosis, or TB. He stayed in a special rest home called a sanatorium. Barbara closed the studio and found a job.

Malak's spirit was strong, and while gaining his strength, he used his time to define what he wanted to do. He decided to take photographs that were personally important. By photographing the landscape of Canada, he would show what his new country meant to him.

A few years later, in 1956, tuberculosis again stopped his work. Barbara got help with their young family and began taking children's portraits to pay the bills. Once he was well, Malak showed the same energy for which his brother was famous. Out with his camera again, Malak stood on logs in rushing rivers and atop mountains to capture in pictures the Canada he loved.

Malak's photographs and books on Canada became well known.

Home at Little Wings

AROUND LITTLE WINGS

The Karshes named their trees after their friends. Two large spruces were called Steichen and Garo, for their favourite photographers. They also had beautiful flower and herb gardens. One day Yousuf spotted a rabbit nibbling some plants. He shook his finger and warned with a smile, "I'll speak to you tomorrow!"

Solange, Aunt Lucia and Malak's wife, Barbara, enjoy a beautiful day at Little Wings.

A year after they were married, Solange and Yousuf began building a house.

In Aleppo, Syria, the Karsh family had lived in a traditional stone building. Inside, apartments ringed a courtyard, where families gathered in the evenings to talk. In Canada, Yousuf built a non-classical house with a middle east feeling. The rooms had high ceilings, and unlike most Canadian homes, the house had a flat roof.

The small house also had an exciting mixture of glass and modern angles. As an artist, Yousuf insisted on large windows so he could enjoy the light and the view. When *Canadian Home Journal* published an article about the building by Solange, people wrote to ask how they could build the same fantastic house.

The unusual house sat near the Rideau River, outside of Ottawa. Birds used the river to guide them with their migration. More than one hundred different kinds of birds visited over the years. Solange and Yousuf called the house Little Wings, in honour of their feathered guests.

The Karshes' beloved cat, Anica

A very spoiled cat lived with the Karshes. When Solange and Yousuf looked for a Persian kitten, Yousuf thought it should be grey so it would show best in photographs. They named their new kitten Anica. Solange explained to a friend that in Arabic this meant "the Honourable Miss So-and-So".

The Karshes taught the playful kitten not to chase birds. Yousuf never had any pets growing up, and he loved Anica very much. Solange complained that he would kiss the cat in the morning before he kissed his wife.

Little Wings was a haven for birds, pets and people. Solange and Yousuf worked very hard and needed a quiet place. Here they could swim, skate, play tennis, go for walks, read, listen to music, cook meals and visit with friends. Little Wings meant so much to the Karshes that they also named one of their photographic companies "Little Wings".

The Scowling British Prime Minister

AT WORK DURING THE WAR

During the Second World War, working and travelling became tricky for Yousuf. Gasoline was hard to come by. Also, with many military people on the move, hotel rooms were scarce. The studio also had troubles with photographic supply companies, which had to give priority to war work, not portraits. Kodak warned that paper was hard to obtain. The studio used resources carefully to produce many photographs of men and women in uniform for their loved ones.

Canada's Houses of Parliament in Ottawa

The time between Yousuf's birthday in late-December and the New Year seemed very lucky for him. For instance, that was the time of year he had first arrived in Canada, and December 30th was the day he took a photograph that changed his life.

During the Second World War, the British prime minister, Winston Churchill, was an important leader of the Allied forces. Yousuf heard this man was coming to Canada. Excitedly, he telephoned Prime Minister King's office. Yousuf learned he would have the chance to make a portrait after Mr. Churchill gave a speech in Parliament.

The nervous photographer prepared the night before, setting up his equipment in a room in the Parliament buildings called the Speaker's Chambers. He found a man about the same size as Churchill and practised lighting. Even so, he couldn't sleep that night. His mind was too busy going over all the details.

On December 30, 1941, Prime Minister Churchill gave a famous speech to the senators and members of parliament. He said the Germans had bragged: "In three weeks, England will have her neck wrung like a chicken." But Britain had not given up so easily. "Some chicken;

Karsh's photograph of Prime Minister Churchill became known as "The Roaring Lion" picture.

some neck!" Churchill crowed triumphantly.

After the speech, the British prime minister was tired and ready to relax. But when he entered the little room where Yousuf waited, bright lights were switched on. Churchill was surprised.

"Sir, I hope I will be fortunate enough to make a portrait of you worthy of this historic occasion," Yousuf said softly.

"Why was I not told?" Churchill thundered. But, puffing on his cigar, he agreed to one photograph.

Yousuf knew that many photographs already showed Churchill with his cigar. He wanted a different pose. Almost without thinking, he went up to the prime minister and respectfully said, "If you please, sir." Yousuf plucked the cigar out of the surprised man's mouth and put it in an ashtray.

Churchill scowled. Yousuf quickly squeezed the bulb for the shutter. Churchill couldn't help laughing at the young man's courage. He allowed another photograph, then told Yousuf, "You can even make a roaring lion stand still to be photographed."

INSPIRING PHOTOGRAPHS

Yousuf photographed the Dutch baby Princess Margriet, who was born safely in Canada during the war. Airplanes dropped thousands of copies of the print over Europe to inspire freedom fighters. Years later, Yousuf met a man who had been a young boy in a prison camp. When the young prisoner saw the photograph on the ground, he hid it. The boy risked death to keep the portrait of the baby that to him was a symbol of life and hope.

Fame

After Yousuf had taken some photos of Prime Ministers King and Churchill together, he hurried to the studio. Would the photographs turn out? Solange thought her worried husband looked like a "small olive, all alone".

While the print was still wet, Yousuf and Solange saw a powerful photograph of a brave and determined Churchill. They started hugging. They knew that the photograph would do well.

They were right. The photograph was first published in *Saturday Night.* Then, *Life* magazine offered $100 to have the photograph on its cover. At the time, it was a lot of money.

In Aleppo, Syria, the day that Yousuf's cover photograph of Churchill appeared, his little brother Salim was home from school. The principal of the school sped over to the Karsh home to show them the magazine. The family was very proud.

Yousuf had made what would become one of the most famous photographs in the world. It is known as "The Roaring Lion".

Yousuf on assignment for *Life* magazine

No Lights in London

Yousuf had photographed Prime Minister Churchill, but he wanted to record more faces of the leaders of the Allied forces. With a helpful letter from Prime Minister King, Yousuf sailed to England in the fall of 1943. On the Atlantic, Yousuf asked the captain what the boat was carrying. "Explosives!" was the answer.

Fortunately, Yousuf and his assistant arrived safely, along with their 180 kilograms, or 400 pounds, of equipment. But in London, Yousuf discovered that some of equipment didn't work with the British electrical system. He scrambled to borrow things. From then on, he brought less when he travelled, rented some items, and left some of his own things with an agent.

London subway stations (called the "Underground" there) were converted into shelters to keep people safe from German bombing. Here people are sleeping on the tracks.

A friend took Yousuf to visit an underground shelter in a subway. The shelters protected people from the bombs that German planes dropped. They were also home for those whose houses had been bombed.

In his little notebook, Yousuf jotted down what he saw. Londoners slept just a few

PLAYWRIGHT

Yousuf's camera caught George Bernard Shaw with an impish smile. When the elderly playwright learned that Yousuf was Armenian, he said, "I have many Armenian friends. The best way to keep the Armenians strong and healthy is to exterminate them every once in a while." Yousuf took what Shaw said in good humour as a joke. Other people found it less funny.

Karsh found the sitting with George Bernard Shaw, a man who wrote many brilliant plays, to be "stimulating". At first Shaw only wanted to give Karsh five minutes of his time, but the session lasted much longer.

metres away from the tracks where the trains rolled by. He was impressed by the children who continued to laugh and play in the terrible conditions.

In Canada, Solange worried. But Yousuf's letters promised her that he had been "born under a lucky star," so all would be well. The lights in London were put out at night so enemy pilots could not see the city. Yousuf told Solange that these blackouts made him think of a happy time in his childhood. He said that using flashlights "in the dark reminds me of Christmas time, when my father led us children, at midnight, to Mass."

In two months, Yousuf and his assistant had photographed more than forty important people. He was tired, but he had wonderful photographs of war leaders, religious men, famous writers and even the king. When people saw his portraits of their heroes in newspapers and magazines, they felt hopeful.

After the war, Yousuf put some of the photographs in a book. He added stories from the notes that Solange had made him write after each sitting. He dedicated his first book, *Faces of Destiny*, published in 1946, to Solange.

Skippy and Yousuf at the U.N.

THE UNITED NATIONS

Fifty countries signed the charter of the United Nations in April 1945. A few months later, the countries approved or "ratified" the charter on October 24, 1945. Around the world, October 24 is called "United Nations Day". People celebrate the work this international organization does in the world for peace, security and human rights.

As the war ended, Yousuf travelled to San Francisco for *Life* magazine. His camera recorded images of the people who created the United Nations. Two lucky high school students assisted Yousuf in April 1945. One of them, fourteen-year-old Skippy Phillips, wrote an essay about his experiences.

The assistants worked hard. They looked after and set up eight cases of equipment. Each day, before the diplomats arrived, the boys prepared the room. After the session, they took everything down. They made sure that the equipment arrived safely at the next hotel, where they would set up again.

Skippy noted that the politicians enjoyed looking at the albums of Yousuf's well-known work. They really liked the photograph of Prime Minister Churchill and the portrait of black American singer and activist Paul Robeson.

The young man was impressed when Yousuf spoke French with some people, then chatted in Arabic with the future king of Saudi Arabia. Ibn Abdul Aziz Faisal told Yousuf he believed more in action than in talk. In his notebook, Yousuf scribbled down the man's thoughts: "Words are like the sand of the desert. They blow

During a photo session with singer-activist Paul Robeson, Karsh asked the man to sing. Perhaps as a result, Robeson looks very relaxed and happy in this portrait.

constantly, but they accomplish very little."

Skippy collected autographs and shook hands with many of the leaders whom people hoped would bring world peace. He told Joseph Bech, from Luxembourg, that he wanted to be a diplomat one day. Bech answered, "I hope that we will do such a good job here, that in twenty-five years there will be no need for diplomats."

These lines end Skippy's essay:

"Mr. Karsh is one man that I shall never forget, for his thoughtfulness, friendliness, and all round niceness. He is truly a great man, and I had the honour of working with him.

So ends the story of an adventure that comes only once in a lifetime, and it came to me at the age of fourteen."

Miss Keller, Miss Taylor and Mr. Einstein

The great scientist Albert Einstein photographed by Karsh in 1948

After the war, Yousuf added movie stars, singers and scientists to the list of people that he had photographed. Sometimes, he decided which people he wanted to photograph. At other times, magazines hired him. Readers wanted to see the portraits and read the interesting stories Yousuf told about meeting the person. The magazine staff might prepare questions for him to ask. He always had something to talk about with his sitters and funny stories to make them smile.

Some of the people Yousuf met were very important to him. He had admired Helen Keller for a long time. Keller could not see, hear, or speak, yet she learned to communicate through sign language. When Yousuf saw Keller, he said, "This is not the first time I have met you." When he was learning English, he had read an inspiring article by Keller called "How to Appreciate a Sunset". Yousuf told Keller that now that he knew her, he thought more about sunrises than sunsets.

Karsh's 1948 photo of Helen Keller (right) and her devoted companion Polly Thompson

A GREAT CANADIAN SINGER

Yousuf photographed Portia White, a famous singer from Nova Scotia. He said she had "a beautiful voice, glorious eyes, a sweet personality, and all the sincerity in the world." White couldn't pay much, but that didn't stop Yousuf from taking "untold pains" the day he photographed her in 1946. The photograph became a stamp in 2000, one of the two dozen Canadian stamps to feature portraits by Karsh of Ottawa.

"Karsh of Ottawa" trademarks were unique lighting and a portrait that included not only a person's face, but also his or her hands. As Yousuf photographed Helen Keller, he felt it was important to suggest the light from within Keller, as well to show her sensitive hands, the way she communicated with the world.

Yousuf met many exciting people who worked in films. In 1946, he photographed teenaged Elizabeth Taylor, who had just acted in a movie about horse riding called *National Velvet*. Yousuf posed Taylor holding a kitten. The next time he saw Taylor, she let him know that she had named the kitten "Michael Karsh Taylor".

In 1948, he photographed one of the greatest scientists of all time, Albert Einstein. Yousuf noted in his book, *Portraits of Greatness,* that Einstein, who had fled from Germany before the war, was "the greatest refugee of our century". Yousuf asked the important man, "To whom should we look for the hope of the world's future?" Einstein replied, "To ourselves." The portrait shows Einstein's dark eyes glowing, perhaps lit by his positive thoughts about humanity.

The "sincerity, charm and the great promise of her wonderful voice" were the things that impressed Karsh about Nova Scotian singer Portia White.

Having Your Portrait Made

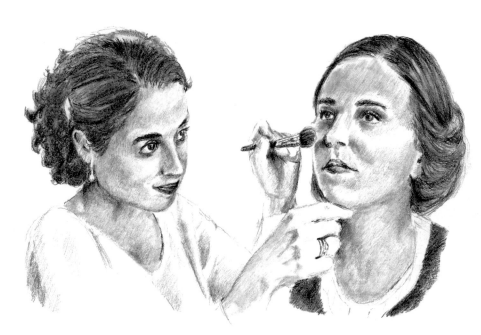

Irene Craig Neil worked as a cashier at the Château Laurier and told the following story. She wanted an exceptional photograph for her husband, who was away in England. Irene saved her money, made matching dresses for herself and her daughter, and went to the Karsh studio.

Inside, the cheerful secretary welcomed mother and daughter as if they were special. As they waited, Irene looked at the photographs of famous people on the walls. Then Solange glided in on soft ballerina shoes. She put some make-up on Irene. Irene thought it looked "ghastly", but under the lights the make-up gave her face a soft look.

Irene found Solange "radiated pride and confidence in her husband's ability..." Already,

WHAT NOT TO DO!

Before the day of the sitting, the studio let clients know how to prepare. Men were told not to have a haircut. Women were asked not to wear dresses with wild prints. Yousuf felt plainer clothes made better photographs and freshly cut or washed hair looked unnatural through the camera's lens.

Karsh's photo of the famous
Canadian humourist Stephen Leacock

A 1946 Karsh portrait of
Canadian figure skater
Barbara Ann Scott

she felt relaxed. When they entered the studio, Yousuf stopped adjusting a lamp. He smiled and bowed "in an old world way".

Behind the camera, he checked the picture through the viewfinder. Because of the laws of optics, what he saw was upside down and backwards! But through experience, Yousuf knew how the finished photograph would look, and how to improve it. He moved the two sitters several times before squeezing the bulb that opened the shutter to record the image.

He spoke to his sitters while he was working. He often surprised them with everything he knew about them. This time he did not speak much. "You can almost feel his intensity as he works," Irene noted. "He dashed from his camera many times to flex our wrists or rearrange our hands."

Yousuf charmed Irene's young daughter, although Irene thought the kind man's accent made some words hard for the child to understand.

"Mr. Karsh," Irene wrote in an article, "achieved wonderful results with his poses of my daughter's small hand resting in mine." Her husband loved the portraits. He wrote "You both appear to be talking to me." Yousuf had found the best way to make the photograph of an ordinary mother and daughter seem special.

The Dark Room
and Beyond

Karsh must have had fun photographing the famous comedy troupe the Marx Brothers (Harpo, Chico and Groucho).

MOMENT OF TRUTH

Yousuf wanted to record the greatness of spirit in each person before his camera. He would often explain, "There is a brief moment when all there is in a man's mind and soul and spirit may be reflected through his eyes, his hands, his attitude. This is the moment to record. This is the elusive 'moment of truth'."

When sitters left the studio, they felt that they had done a good job. But the important part of the work was just beginning.

Technicians helped develop the glass plates or film and some test photographs. In the dark room, a red light let the technicians see, but did not spoil the negatives or the paper on which the negatives would be printed. In several chemical baths, the image was fixed on the negative. When dried, the negative was exposed or "printed" onto the paper, then fixed in another chemical bath and allowed to dry.

Yousuf might view the test print and find too much shadow near the nose or an ugly dot on the person's chin. Special retouching pencils and tools would correct the problem.

When the proofs were ready, clients ordered the ones they liked best. Soon they would have a wonderful portrait signed by Karsh of Ottawa.

Citizen of Canada

The Second World War helped Canada develop from a British colony into a more independent country. It was time to show this shift. With the Canadian Citizenship Act, the people of Canada, except for First Nations peoples, would no longer be citizens of Britain, but of Canada.

Politicians and some specially selected immigrants, such as Yousuf, were the first to receive the new citizenship certificates. Yousuf was a British subject of Armenian birth living in Canada. His status changed on January 3, 1947 at a special event, the first Canadian Citizenship ceremony.

Yousuf (top row, right) at the citizenship ceremony with other new Canadians

The night was snowy, but the music and red coats of the RCMP band set a cheery mood at the Supreme Court building. The candidates from Romania, Italy, Estonia and other countries took their seats on benches at the front of the room. The crowd in the Great Chamber hushed as the speeches began. Resting his fingers together, Yousuf listened intently. All of Canada could hear the ceremony through a special radio broadcast.

WHAT IS CITIZENSHIP?

The 1982 Canadian Charter of Rights and Freedoms gives Canadian citizens the right to: live and work anywhere in the country; a fair trial; protection against discrimination and special First Nations peoples' rights. Canadians also have freedom of thought, speech, religion and peaceful assembly. Some of the responsibilities of citizens are to vote, help the community, obey laws, respect the rights of others and help to end discrimination.

Dressed in scarlet robes, Chief Justice Rinfret spoke in English and French. He said different groups made Canada strong. Canada had "accepted the gifts" from each "and made them into an enduring heritage." He informed those about to take their oaths that they would have benefits as well as responsibilities. Then, one by one, the candidates promised to serve the king and to "faithfully obey the laws of Canada and fulfill my duties as a Canadian citizen."

Prime Minister King was the first to receive his certificate, and Yousuf was tenth. Yousuf joked that if he put his thumb over the "0" on his certificate, that he was Number One.

The ceremony ended as the bells in the Peace Tower rang out. Then the private parties began. Uncle George and his wife, Aunt Florence, had come from Montreal. Solange wrote to friends that they celebrated into "the wee small hours".

In Syria, Yousuf's family was very happy. No one was more elated than Yousuf. Being part of the first citizenship ceremony in Canada was a great honour that he would cherish his whole life.

Yousuf listens carefully during the ceremony.

A Day of Tremendous Joy

The Karsh family had long dreamed of being together in Canada. They hoped to have good jobs, and to be somewhere where they believed terrible things would never again happen to Armenians. Yousuf had not seen his parents and brother Jamil for more than twenty years. He had never met his youngest brother, Salim, who was born in 1925. One can imagine how much Yousuf wanted to hug his mother, to listen to his father's funny stories and to hear about his brothers' dreams for the future.

But there was a big problem. His mother Bahia had an eye disease that affected many Armenian survivors, and people with trachoma were not permitted into Canada. Fortunately, as a medical student, brother Jamil knew people who could help, and eventually Bahia was cured.

Another challenge worried Yousuf. How would his parents fit into life in Canada? They didn't speak English or French. Yousuf was so busy working that he was afraid that his parents would be lonely.

Proud Mrs. Karsh poses with her sons: Yousuf, Bahia and Jamil (front), Salim and Malak (back)

ARMENIANS COMING TO CANADA

Getting immigration papers isn't like getting an invitation to someone's house. You can't call and ask to come over. Solange's letters often spoke about the challenges. In the 1920s, Canada did not welcome many people from the Middle East. During the 1930s, many Canadians were out of work, and Canada didn't need immigrant workers. In the 1940s, Canada helped people from countries most affected by the Second World War. Syria, where the Karshes lived, was not included.

Some members of the family had an idea. The newly arriving members could live near Bahia's sister, Lucia, and other relatives in Sainte-Marie-de-Beauce, in the province of Quebec. Youngest brother Salim could live there too and help the Karsh parents adjust. As for Jamil, Yousuf had been paying his studies in medicine at the American University of Beirut in Lebanon. Jamil would continue his education and become a doctor, as Yousuf had once dreamed of doing.

The letter of permission finally arrived, and the family was on their way.

On July 1, 1948, their ship entered New York harbour. As a surprise, Uncle George and Yousuf had a little boat take them to meet the family before their ship docked. There was great happiness when they finally met.

Soon after, the family flew to Montreal. It was the parents' first time in an airplane and part of their great adventure.

Canadians celebrated July 1, 1948, as Canada's eighty-first birthday. To Yousuf, it would be remembered as a day of "tremendous joy".

The famous Statue of Liberty in New York harbour is an important symbol of the hope of immigrants for a better life in North America.

Different Work

ASSISTING THE MASTER

As Yousuf worked, an assistant helped place the equipment, fix the lights and perform many other tasks.

Sometimes an assistant would take the place of the sitter so Yousuf could try different lighting and poses. The assistant might be standing in for the president of France or the prime minister of Canada. Usually Yousuf had a professional assistant, but sometimes a taxi driver or a passerby was talked into helping.

The family settled in, and Yousuf continued his work. From his first days in photography, Yousuf had wanted to make portraits of interesting people. Now he began trying different sorts of challenging portrait work, some of it in factories.

The Atlas Steel Company hired Yousuf to photograph their workers in Welland, Ontario for a calendar. Atlas had manufactured metal products such as gun parts for the war. By 1950, the factories focused on stainless steel for peacetime uses.

Yousuf visited the foundry to choose the people and places for the photographs. Solange wrote down the life stories of the men, many of whom came from other countries. The photography was challenging. The foundry was a noisy, hot and dangerous place. His assistant had to protect him from flying sparks. One camera lens began to melt from the heat. Yet Yousuf was able to capture the workers on film.

Karsh called this photo of an Atlas Steel worker "Lancelot".

Across Canada

ON THE ROAD

Yousuf often travelled away from Ottawa because he always tried to take photographs of people in their own setting: their home or workplace. That meant he had to visit many points of the globe for his job. He would spend months of each year on the road. Crazy schedules had him going from Boston in the east one day to Los Angeles in the west the next day.

Karsh photographed these two boys in Newfoundland in 1951.

Yousuf travelled across his adopted land in the early 1950s, photographing Canadian cities for *Maclean's* magazine. It gave him a chance to try on some spiffy new hats! Yousuf usually wore a suit and a black hat. At the Calgary Stampede, he was given a snazzy white cowboy hat to go on his balding head.

Yousuf worked long into the night on the photographs of Canadian cities. He developed film in the bathroom of the hotel room as Solange typed. Her notes helped create articles that went with Yousuf's photographs.

One article described the "worst" meal the Karshes ever had. In Charlottetown, Prince Edward Island, Solange and Yousuf didn't like one potato dish. But potatoes were the pride of the province, and the members of parliament from P.E.I. were upset. They discussed the article in Parliament in December 1952. Mr. McClure, a member of parliament, rudely called Karsh a "foreigner—who is now a doubtful Canadian".

A huge debate began in newspapers across the country. Some letter writers did not like immigrants, but most people supported new Canadians. Many articles said McClure had made a mistake. The leader of the Conservative Party apologized.

Books and Portraits of Greatness

Pope Pius XII

THE POPE

Yousuf met the pope three times. He had never dreamed he would meet the head of the Roman Catholic Church, let alone photograph him. The first pope he photographed, Pope Pius XII, blessed some items for Yousuf in 1949. One little medal he gave to his father. Amish was thrilled.

In 1957, Yousuf worked on a book titled *This is the Mass* with his friend, Fulton Sheen, a man who would become an archbishop in the Roman Catholic Church. Yousuf enjoyed doing photographs for four books on Catholicism.

In 1959, Solange and Yousuf published a book called *Portraits of Greatness*. Its photographs became the first one-man photography exhibition at the National Gallery of Canada in Ottawa.

When Yousuf's work was shown across the country, the large prints amazed Canadians. They admired the portraits of the people who made a difference in their lives: Prime Minister Louis St. Laurent (1953), pianist Glenn Gould (1957), Nobel Prize winner Dr. Charles H. Best (1958) and others.

As Yousuf's exhibitions toured the world, visitors were excited by the photographer's views of actor Audrey Hepburn (1956), filmmaker Walt Disney (1956), India's prime minister Jawaharlal Nehru (1956), and by a very sensitive portrait of author Ernest Hemingway (1957).

Slow Down!

CHARACTER

Yousuf loved the challenge of portrait photography. He photographed faces and hands, but he also hinted at what the sitter's spirit was like. He knew that some of his subjects had come through many hardships stronger than before. "Character," he said, "is like a photograph. It develops in the dark."

Yousuf put huge amounts of energy into his work. In July 1959, he was dashing around Washington photographing American politicians when he felt pains in his chest. Doctors discovered he'd had a heart attack.

In hospital, he received hundreds of get well cards. Senator John F. Kennedy, a future American president, was one of Yousuf's many photographic subjects who sent good wishes.

When he returned home, Yousuf needed to rest. For the first time in the busy man's life, he had a vacation at Little Wings. He read, listened to music and visited with his many friends. By autumn, Yousuf was much better and back at the work he loved. He told a friend, "I must continue to love the same way of life but love it less fervently." In other words, he wanted to continue with photography, but he knew he had to slow down.

Karsh's photo of future American president John F. Kennedy

68

Losing Solange

A 1938 photo of Solange
by Karsh titled
"Spring Song"

Solange thought Yousuf loved his work too much. After he bought a new camera lens, she teased, "I didn't marry a man. I married a camera with an Ektar lens for a heart." Nonetheless, Solange helped her "great little man" all she could.

As Yousuf's business manager, she ran the busy studio. She looked after the details of trips, right down to having coins in her pocket to tip bellboys. Solange did a lot of Yousuf's writing: she typed up notes after sittings, wrote the first draft of some books and prepared material for what she hoped would one day be Yousuf's biography.

Around the time Yousuf had his heart attack in Washington, Solange, at home in Ottawa, learned that she had cancer. She waited a little while before telling her ill husband the bad news.

Solange fought the cancer for a few years. In January 1961, Yousuf was on his way to Chicago when he received a telegram. Solange needed him. He returned to be with her. She died on January 26, 1961. As she wished, Solange died at Little Wings, surrounded by love.

A MAGIC FRIEND

While Solange was ill, Yousuf brought her a puppy. He had a plane ticket for his "young friend", but the airline people didn't want the dog to sit with him. Finally, they let the pup stay in the area with the coats. The bubbly black poodle was called Clicquot, the name of a French champagne. Yousuf said, "I feel that all of us must have a pet, and to have a dog you have acquired a friend."

Yousuf felt so sad, he could hardly speak. Joyce Large was Solange's friend and secretary of the Karsh studio. She answered seven hundred letters, many of them from the Karshes' famous friends. Joyce wrote, "We cannot ever forget the unique part (Solange) played in the life of Yousuf." Joyce added that Solange had faith in Yousuf even in the "early days".

Yousuf would remember Solange in many ways. Because she was an actor and director, Yousuf began the Solange Karsh Award for the best one act play through the Ottawa Little Theatre. The prize medal bore a beautiful portrait Karsh had made of Solange dancing.

The doctor ordered Yousuf to take some holidays. But, Joyce knew Yousuf would soon return to the work. Joyce told their agent in Britain, Mr. Blau, that she already had "a heavy program planned for him." She knew Yousuf had "strength that will spur him to even greater accomplishments..."

Yousuf with his friend Clicquot

70

Changing Family

Yousuf had fun dancing with his niece Marianne, Malak and Barbara's daughter.

Yousuf loved children, although he never had any. However, he played a big role in the lives of his family. By telephone, he often checked on his parents in Sainte-Marie-de-Beauce. He sent money to ensure they had everything they needed. Bahia's sister, Aunt Lucia, and her son lived nearby and they helped make the transition easier.

Salim stayed near his parents and began a career in retail, first working at a cousin's store. Soon married and the father of two children, he was a beloved member of his new community and worked hard as a volunteer.

Yousuf helped his brother Jamil to continue his education in medicine. He had paid for some of Jamil's schooling in Beirut, Lebanon. In North America, Yousuf wrote letters to find Jamil a place to intern. Jamil later worked in Waterbury, Connecticut, in the U.S.

Malak stayed in Ottawa with Barbara and their four children. His business as a landscape photographer grew until he, too, was famous.

SALIM'S RECIPE

The Karshes loved sharing special food with family and friends. This recipe is translated and adapted from a book by Salim.

Hummus

Mix together with a mixer or food processor:

1 can chick peas
25 ml tahini (sesame seed paste)
45 ml olive oil
15 ml cumin
15 ml salt
1 pinch cayenne pepper
Sprinkle chopped parsley on top.
Serve with crackers or bread.

Yousuf was glad to have the chance to cherish his parents as they grew older. However, gentle, brown-eyed Bahia died in 1958. She was remembered as a woman of great faith. When father Amish died in June 1962, big brother Yousuf was considered to be the head of the Karsh family.

Yousuf and the others were happy to be on the same side of the ocean, where they could be close enough to visit. In winter, they got together around Christmas. In summer, they had barbecues at Little Wings. Salim remembers that when they saw one another, they affectionately called each other "brother", or "khyao". Yousuf delighted in his nephews and nieces. They knew Uncle Yousuf was there to help, and also to have fun.

Yousuf and his uncle George Nakash enjoying a barbecue

72

Yousuf's Little Star

Estrellita in a photograph by Yousuf

Yousuf had been on his way to Chicago to photograph Dr. Walter C. Alvarez when the trip was cancelled because of Solange's illness.

Dr. Alvarez was called "America's Family Doctor". He gave advice to people through newspaper columns and books. He was helped by a talented medical writer and editor with a lively sense of humour named Estrellita Nachbar. Estrellita means "little star".

When the short, balding photographer finally came to take her boss's picture, Estrellita wasn't excited about meeting him. But magic happened. One newspaper said, "Something clicked more than the shutter." First Estrellita noticed Yousuf's great, brown eyes. Perhaps Yousuf warmed to Miss Nachbar's smiling face. Yousuf found Estrellita could really make him laugh.

Yousuf and Estrellita attended a Balinese dance and other events together. They shared many interests. Yousuf had wanted to be a doctor, and Estrellita was a medical writer. They both loved helping young people. Before long, Estrellita was planning her wedding dress and being baptized so they could be married in a Catholic church.

ESTRELLITA

Newspapers and magazines were soon reporting that Estrellita was born in 1930 to Philip Nachbar and Rachel Levi. She grew up in New Jersey, U.S., and studied at Antioch College, Ohio, in the U.S. One summer, she worked at a camp for children with cerebral palsy and was also involved with the National Society for Crippled Children and Adults. She never lost her interest in children or in medicine, or her great sense of humour.

The wedding was a special day, just for Yousuf and Estrellita and a few friends. Yousuf's friend, Bishop Sheen, performed the mass at St. Patrick's Cathedral in New York on August 28, 1962.

Estrellita found out right away how busy and exciting life with Yousuf would be. She had packed clothes for a honeymoon on the windy Atlantic coast of Canada. But plans changed, and the new bride found herself in the hot climate of Rome, Italy, shopping for something cool enough to wear.

Estrellita and Yousuf on their wedding day

Russia

RUSSIAN DOLLS

The Russians gave Estrellita a large matrushka doll, a wooden doll with fifteen smaller ones inside. "I am a child about dolls," Estrellita laughed. She presented the lovely doll to the Children's Hospital of Eastern Ontario, in Ottawa. There, sick children and their visitors can marvel at the brightly painted dolls, each one, from the smallest to the largest, different from her sisters.

Estrellita and the Soviet minister of culture with a matrushka doll

Life was exciting for Yousuf and Estrellita, as they travelled to many places. In the 1960s, more and more of the world became the professional home of Karsh of Ottawa.

In April 1963, they travelled to Russia. At that time, the communist party was in power. The government did not have many contacts with non-communist governments. Relations were very tense between the U.S. and Russia (then called the U.S.S.R.) during this period, known as the Cold War. However, Yousuf was a Canadian photographer, and not a citizen of the United States. He was the first photographer from the Western world to be allowed to photograph important Soviet Russians. People excitedly awaited Yousuf's photographs.

Yousuf made a famous portrait of the head of the government, Chairman Nikita Khrushchev. In the photograph, Khrushchev seems a little fierce, but he also has twinkly eyes and a warm smile. He looks like an Arctic explorer dressed in a great fur coat.

The fur coat was Yousuf's idea. But April can be hot in Russia, and Khrushchev's aides were against using the heavy coat. However, Khrushchev agreed to put the coat on. Before the historic photograph was taken, Khrushchev warned, "Be quick, or this snow leopard will devour me."

CELEBRITIES, 1960 TO 1970

How many famous people could Yousuf's camera see in ten years? From 1960 to 1970, he made portraits of the heads of government of Egypt, France, Germany, India and Russia. During this time, he also photographed five American presidents and two Canadian prime ministers (Lester B. Pearson and Pierre Elliott Trudeau). He also found time to photograph Martin Luther King and the crew of Apollo XI.

New Adventures

Yousuf was fifty-five years old in 1963, but once more he was ready to take on new challenges. He tried an exciting kind of portrait work on film sets. Film companies hired the famous photographer to create portraits of their stars to use in ads. Yousuf travelled to South Africa to take pictures of the shooting of the movie *Zulu.* He found working outdoors with natural light tricky, but he loved his time in South Africa and the people there.

Yousuf also took photographs of the actors in the movie *Planet of the Apes.* The first set of portraits shows the actors as they looked every day. In the next set, the actors are dressed as the characters in the film. When Yousuf began as a photographer, he could not have imagined that one day he would take photographs of human monkeys.

Dashing Canadian prime minister Pierre Elliott Trudeau

Karsh photographed prime minister Lester B. Pearson in the Houses of Parliament.

76

WORLD FAIRS

Since the first world fair in London in 1851, fascinating creations have been built. The Eiffel Tower was built in Paris for the 1891 exhibition, and the ferris wheel invented for the 1893 fair in Chicago. For Expo '67, modern-looking buildings were constructed at the Montreal site, including the futuristic-looking American pavilion, a twenty-storey glass and steel dome.

Expos in Canada and Japan

In 1967, people from many countries came to Montreal to a huge international fair called Expo '67. The exhibition travels to promote global communication, a goal Yousuf supported. His work had first been shown at the Brussels fair of 1958, but it had a very important place at Expo '67. He was the only person to have his own photography exhibit. The one hundred photographs, "Men Who Make Our World", later travelled to cities all over the globe.

When Expo was held in Osaka, Japan in 1970, Yousuf had the role of photographic advisor. The year before the fair, he and Estrellita travelled to Japan to prepare. On this trip, Yousuf photographed some of the beloved writers and other creative people of the country.

Canada was proud to host Expo '67 in Montreal.
Some of the spectacular buildings can still be seen today.

One person who came before his lens was a Bunraku puppeteer. These artists work together to move very large puppets. The magic puppets seem to cry or to dance a fierce lion dance, as a narrator tells their story over a backdrop of music. Estrellita and Yousuf thought they were very lucky to see where the puppets were made, and to have a special performance. The Karshes enjoyed their tour of Japan very much. Yousuf wrote to a friend that he and Estrellita loved visiting the "shrines and gardens not normally open to Westerners".

A Bunraku puppet

As in many countries, the people of Japan loved the famous photographer's work. His "In Search of Greatness" exhibit toured Japan in 1970. People flocked to the giant Seibu Department Store Gallery to see it. Yousuf's 1962 biography, also called *In Search of Greatness,* translated into Japanese, appeared that year. He had had many great opportunities in his life, and the photographer often saw his photographs in magazines in different languages. Just think what a feeling it would be to see the story of your life written in a language you do not read. Yousuf's skill had brought him worldwide fame and recognition beyond what he ever dreamed.

New Home in a Hotel

The Château Laurier photographed in the 1920s. The hotel is one of Ottawa's most famous landmarks.

CHÂTEAU LAURIER

In 1936, when Yousuf had his first solo exhibit at the Château Laurier, he did not know that one day the hotel would name a room after him. Room 358 in the hotel is known as the Karsh Room to honour the years that Estrellita and Yousuf lived and worked at the hotel. His stunning photographs hang in the suite he occupied and also near the entry to the grand hotel.

After 1973, Yousuf's Sparks Street studio closed, and another one opened in a hotel, also in Ottawa. The Château Laurier is an historic hotel near the Parliament buildings and the beautiful Rideau Canal, where boats float in summer and skaters flit by in winter.

The studio almost fit into its new address, but the huge enlarger, the piece of equipment that made the large prints the studio was known for, was too tall. A hole had to be cut in the ceiling. It was good that their friends upstairs at CBC Radio did not mind.

Sometimes Yousuf stayed in New York, where he had a small studio. For the rest of the year after 1980, when the Karshes were not travelling, they lived at the Château Laurier. They had a new family, the staff of the hotel. Workers stopped by to chat or to ask Estrellita for help with problems in their love lives.

Studio Family

MORE SEVENTIES CELEBRITIES
In the 1970s, Yousuf photographed the men and women who would hold the title of prime minister: Zulfikar Ali Bhutto of Pakistan, Margaret Thatcher of the United Kingdom, and Joe Clark of Canada. Canadian authors Margaret Atwood and Robertson Davies, were topics in 1979, as well as the American artist Andy Warhol.

Yousuf was not always in Ottawa to give instructions, yet he expected the best from his studio team. Mary Alderman began as the secretary of the new studio. Right away, she felt like she was part of a warm, hard-working family. She and the technicians sometimes stayed long hours, but everyone talked and laughed together. Yousuf often tried to give a hand with problems, saying, "Let Poppa help with that."

Mary worked at the studio until it closed in 1992. In those twenty years, there were many last-minute changes, because Yousuf travelled so much. Mary never seemed to mind, and Yousuf called her "unflappable".

Another worker also stayed until the studio closed. Printer Ignas Gabalis was born in Lithuania and came to Canada via Denmark. In 1953, he worked for Malak, then switched to Yousuf's studio. Ignas always tried to make perfect prints. Yousuf called him the "slowest printer in the world". But he knew that this was because Ignas was dedicated to quality.

A contact sheet, or mini-prints that would be used to select larger prints, showing a busy day at the studio. With digital cameras, photographers can see what the photograph will look like before it is printed.

INDUSTRY CHANGES

Now we know that some chemicals the photography industry used were toxic. Technicians and printers didn't always put on protective aprons and gloves when working with these chemicals. Later in life, Ignas had kidney problems, perhaps in part because of the side effects of years of chemical use. He didn't know how important it was to wear proper protection.

Ignas made a special "recipe", or formula for toning his prints by using gold chloride. Before fixing the prints, Ignas placed them in this toner so that they would have a rich, warm purply-brown colour when they dried. The toner was difficult to make and hard to use. But the Karsh studio always used the best materials.

When the studio was not too busy, Ignas's ten-year-old daughter, Sonja, helped make test prints. In the dark room, she was thrilled to see the images appear as if "by magic". The wet prints then went to the drying machine. The huge steel drum was heated, and the prints were affixed to it to dry as the drum turned. Sonja waited until an empty place came by, then she put a print on. She loved this job.

Sonja knew Ignas was proud when he saw his name in one of Yousuf's books. She also liked hearing her quiet father talk excitedly when someone important, such as Prince Charles, came to be photographed at the Château Laurier.

Yousuf and Ignas Gabalis hard at work

MUSCULAR DYSTROPHY

Muscular dystrophy, or MD, is a group of diseases that has no cure. Some types affect children. Each type of MD is caused by a defect in a gene that causes the loss of a protein that muscles need or has another damaging effect on muscle tissue. Bodies need muscles to help them crawl, sit, stand, breathe and keep the heart beating. In some cases, people with MD die while still young. In other cases, people with MD live long lives and adapt to what their bodies can do.

Famous comedian Jerry Lewis sits with Paul Hawkins and perhaps thinks about the future of children, such as Paul, who cope with MD.

The Empty Spot

An advertisement in *Time* magazine in 1981 showed portraits of Yousuf's gallery of famous people. One spot remained empty. Yousuf told the world he had never met this special person. Yousuf was reserving the space "for the person who discovers the cure for muscular dystrophy".

Estrellita had spent time at a camp for children with disabilities. She was aware of the problems young people with MD had. Yousuf had wanted to become a doctor to help people. As a gifted photographer, he knew he could help the team fighting MD. He did not usually photograph children, but for many years, beginning in 1963, he gave his time and talent to the cause. He photographed the child chosen to represent all children with MD. The photographs were used on posters to help raise money.

One photograph of a boy, Paul Hawkins, in a wheelchair catches him having a quiet moment with Jerry Lewis. Lewis is the famous comedian who championed the MD campaign.

Yousuf found the MD poster children were lit with "faith in the goodness of life..." He said, "This makes the rest of us redouble our efforts to translate their faith into reality." Estrellita and Yousuf saw the Solange Gauthier-Karsh Laboratory open in 1995 at the Children's Hospital of Eastern Ontario in Ottawa. Research could be carried out on Duchenne muscular dystrophy and Becker muscular dystrophy that affects young males.

Ben Teraberry

CHILDREN AS PHOTOGRAPHERS

Yousuf thought that cameras were great tools and toys for children. He once wrote "...children from the age of five on can learn to handle simple box cameras; and they can experience that unique sense of magic which never fails to baffle even hardened and saddened grown-ups when hey, presto, there appears an exact likeness of Mummy, Daddy or the boy next door."

MERITORIOUS SERVICE

Important events were happening for Yousuf. His book *Faces of our Time* had come out, and he had a one-man exhibit at the International Center of Photography in New York. But the most important event was in 1971, when he received the United States Presidential Citation for meritorious service to the handicapped for photographing the Annual Poster Child for the Muscular Dystrophy Association.

Ben and other MD ambassadors inspired Yousuf with their strength and courage.

The bright lights and attention at the photography sitting made the 1985–1986 poster child feel nervous. But Yousuf treated Ben Teraberry compassionately. Yousuf asked Ben to play his saxophone. "Top of the class!" he approved. Ben's blue eyes beamed.

Yousuf also gave Ben a chance to be the photographer.

"You tell me what you want me to do," Yousuf-the-subject encouraged Ben-the-photographer.

"Smile," the boy whispered shyly.

"Smile? That's not easy!" Yousuf teased.

Ben squeezed the bulb that closed the shutter and made the photograph.

Giving Back

TEACHING

Yousuf wanted to help students as he had been helped. He taught university courses in Ohio, and gave workshops for his friend the famous landscape photographer Ansel Adams in California. He also went to the Brooks Institute in California to offer students there the chance to assist the best in the business.

One student he chose, Jerry Fielder, arrived in Ottawa from California without even a winter coat. But Fielder wasn't planning on staying. He had come to tell Yousuf in person that he could not accept the offer to be his assistant. However, Jerry was "just charmed" by the warm, friendly Karshes and could not leave. He stayed and eventually became the curator of the Karsh photographs.

Yousuf was a proud citizen of Canada and also part of the global community. One of the responsibilities of a Canadian citizen is to help those in their community. Through his actions, he generously gave back to Canada and the world and added to the great achievements of his life.

Yousuf never forgot being a newcomer in Canada, and he helped immigrants in different ways. Many people who hoped to come to North America contacted the famous Mr. Karsh. Sometimes Yousuf gave money or advice. But he could not save the world one person at a time. He always found a way to use his talents to aid many people. For example, when the Canadian Armenian Congress was founded in 1948 to help Armenian immigrants, Yousuf became its honourary chairperson. Above all, he believed that rather than remembering old hatred, people should work towards the future.

Yousuf's photo of his friend Ansel Adams

Celebrating Karsh

CAKE AND CANDY

Yousuf could be a big kid about cake and candy. When a candy village was set up in the lobby of the Château Laurier at Easter, Yousuf could barely resist taking a nibble from a chocolate bunny or a bite of a yellow marzipan duck.

Every December the hotel's pastry chef would deliver a specially Heavenly Light Lemon Cake to the Karsh suite, along with a Happy Birthday song. One year, Estrellita had a birthday party for her husband. She decorated the table with mice on skis and pencils dressed as toy soldiers. Yousuf had never had a birthday party while growing up.

When people think of a famous figure of the twentieth century, it is often a Karsh photo that comes to mind. With such a long career in portrait photography, museums and galleries around the world marked special Karsh anniversaries.

Important exhibits have celebrated his seventy-fifth, eightieth and ninetieth birthdays in countries such as Germany, Australia, England and Canada. Queen Elizabeth II attended one show called "Karsh in London" in 1998. At the time, Yousuf was ninety and had retired from his sixty-plus-year career. He had just moved to Boston, the city where he had once studied.

Lasting Record

PRESERVING FOR THE FUTURE

The cameras, brushes, enlargers and other items need to be in the climate controlled buildings of the Canada Science and Technology Museum. If they weren't, they might be affected by rust, insects, mould, bright lights or changes in temperature or humidity. An online exhibit of Yousuf's equipment can be viewed at www.sciencetech.technomuses.ca

Yousuf made a great contribution to global culture. He had eleven thousand sittings and helped create more than a dozen books. His work forms a very precious legacy.

Beginning in 1987, the Library and Archives Canada became the home of the studio's prints and 370,000 negatives.

Visitors are asked to wear gloves to look at these negatives and prints so the oil on their fingers does not cause any damage. The special conditions at their new home keep the negatives and prints safe. Fragile glass-plate negatives were used before the 1940s, mixed with cellulose nitrate negatives from 1933 to 1937, and followed by safety film that was less flammable than the earlier cellulose nitrate negatives. All are stored in boxes made out of acid-free materials to help preserve them.

Yousuf began using colour in 1947, and the colour negatives are kept in cold temperatures so the colours do not change. They must be slowly warmed up from -18°C every time someone wishes to see them. With this care, years from now Karsh photographs will look much like the day he took them.

Kenojuak Ashevak

86

Ossip Zadkine

Not everyone can travel to Ottawa, Ontario, and Gatineau, Quebec, to the Library and Archives Canada, so the LAC created a tribute at their www.collectionscanada.ca website **(http://www.collectionscanada.gc.ca/ karsh/index-e.html)**. Here you can look at an alphabet of Yousuf's photographs, from A to Z, from Inuit printmaker Kenojuak Ashevak to Russian-born French sculptor Ossip Zadkine.

The world is fortunate that Karsh's work and the tools that created it are protected. In 1997, the studio's photographic equipment was moved to the Canada Museum of Science and Technology in Ottawa. Anyone who wants can ask to visit Yousuf's cameras, lenses, tripods or the giant enlarger. He could never say which camera he used in any one shot, but the museum will preserve all of them so that even future generations will be able to see Yousuf's favourite Graflex 4 x 5 camera or his main Calumet Company 8 x 10 camera.

Honours

BELOVED OF OTTAWA

Ottawa presented Yousuf and Malak with keys to the city in 2000, and it still has a special place for the two brothers who gave so much to Canada's capital. The city gives a Karsh Award for outstanding artistic work in a photo-based medium. If you go to the area today, you might see an art show at the Karsh-Masson Gallery (Masson was also an artist); drive down Karsh Drive or Malak Street; or play at Karsh Park.

Karsh in Ottawa, 1991

From his first photography prize in 1926, honours drifted into Yousuf's life like lovely snowflakes. Artistic and photographic societies from as far away as the Czech Republic gave him top awards. The Royal Canadian Academy of Arts selected him as the first photographer to receive its medal; the Professional Photographers of Canada called him Honorary Master of Photographic Arts; the Royal Photographic Society of Britain made him a "fellow".

Although he never finished high school, Yousuf accepted more than eight honorary degrees from universities across North America. When the University of Syracuse gave him a doctorate degree, they thanked him for his gift to the world: "A wonderful photo album of the human family".

The way he used his talents reflected his great heart, and he received more than a dozen major awards. For example, in 1989, he received the Gold Medal of the Americas Society for furthering Canadian-American understanding. In 1990, the Governor General of Canada gave him the Companion of the Order of Canada. This recognizes a life of outstanding work serving Canada or all humanity.

No wonder someone once joked to Yousuf that "one could make a career out of congratulating you." From a teenager hoping to make money to help his family, he had become a figure important to the world.

Still Helping Children

GIFTS TO BOSTON

Yousuf retired to Boston, the city of his apprenticeship, in 1997. Yousuf and Estrellita started the Karsh Prize in Photography and helped the Museum of Fine Arts promote learning about photography with education and a special curator. Some portraits by Karsh of Ottawa are at the museum. Others hang at the Brigham and Women's Hospital in Boston and are admired by patients, staff and visitors there.

The Karsh brothers lived long lives. Malak died in 2001 at age eighty-six and Jamil in July 2, 2002 at age eighty-two. After becoming ill, Yousuf died in Boston on July 13, 2002 at age ninety-three. A Mass was celebrated in Yousuf's memory at Notre-Dame Cathedral in Ottawa. His remains rest at Notre-Dame Cemetery, near the grave of Prime Minister Sir Wilfrid Laurier.

Some time before he died, Yousuf and Estrellita talked about their shared interest in medicine. Yousuf had photographed many doctors. Sometimes he and Estrellita had even watched operations. They also loved helping children, so in September 2005, Estrellita gave twenty of Yousuf's favourite photographs to the Children's Hospital of Eastern Ontario.

At a ceremony, a surprise was announced. CHEO was giving its Emergency Department a new name— the Estrellita and Yousuf Karsh Emergency Department. There would be special training for the staff; new equipment that would help sick children and much more.

Yousuf took this photograph of First Nations boys with TB (see page 46) in an Alberta hospital. The background is a mix of light and shadow, while the boys' faces show both curiosity and bravery. Karsh wanted to do everything possible to help sick children.

A self-portrait, 1956

Estrellita proudly talked about their amazing gift. She knew Yousuf had loved his adopted country, where he had first felt "the sunshine of freedom". "So, it is fitting," she said, "that, from the little boy of nearly a century ago who never had a real childhood, should come a legacy to the children of today, ensuring compassionate care when the need is most urgent."

Yousuf's portraits of well-known people have a place in the Estrellita and Yousuf Karsh Emergency Department. There is the portrait of Winston Churchill that began Yousuf's fame, a playful photograph of filmmaker Walt Disney and a colourful one of skater Karen Magnussen. There is also a photograph titled "Eva and Ava from the National Ballet". The two young dancers were not famous when Yousuf took their photograph, but their thoughtful pose suggests a hopefulness that can inspire other children.

Young people can also see Karsh of Ottawa photographs in galleries and museums in Australia, Germany, Japan and many places across North America. Whether they are of great people, or people in whom Yousuf's camera saw the greatness, the photographs make us stop and think how wonderful each person can be.

Yousuf Karsh's Life and Times

1908, December 23	Yousuf Karsh is born in Mardin, Turkey.
Exact date unknown	The family escapes to Aleppo, Syria, perhaps by 1922.
1924, January 1	Yousuf clears the immigration facility at Pier 2, Halifax, Nova Scotia. His uncle and photographer George Nakash, takes him to Sherbrooke, Quebec.
1926	Wins first prize in a photography contest.
1928	Goes to Boston, Massachusetts, U.S.A., to study with photographer John Garo for three years.
1932	Moves to Ottawa, Ontario. Works for photographer John Powis and soon takes over the Sparks Street Studio.
1933	Attends a play at the Ottawa Little Theatre. Meets Solange Gauthier. Becomes the official photographer for the Dominion Drama Festival.
1936	Appointed as official photographer to the governor general.
1937	Photograph wins the Beautiful Child contest. Brother Malak arrives in Canada.
1939	Marries Solange Gauthier. World War II begins.
1941	Moves to house he calls Little Wings. Photographs British Prime Minister Churchill, creating one of the most famous portraits of all time.
1943	Photographs the King, wartime leaders and people of note in London, England.
1945	Makes portraits of the leaders at the creation of the United Nations. World War II ends.
1946	Portia White and Elizabeth Taylor are among Karsh of Ottawa's subjects. First book, *Faces of Destiny,* is published.
1947	Takes part in the first Canadian citizenship ceremony.
1948	Bahia, Amish, Jamil and Salim Karsh immigrate to Canada. The Canadian Armenian Congress is founded, and Yousuf becomes its honorary president.
1957	*This is the Mass* is published with Karsh of Ottawa photographs.
1959	Yousuf suffers a heart attack. *Portraits of Greatness* is published.
1961	Solange dies of cancer.
1962	Yousuf marries Estrellita Nachbar. *In Search of Greatness: Reflections of Yousuf Karsh* is published.
1963	Begins photographing the poster children of the Muscular Dystrophy Association. Works in Russia and South Africa.
1967	Has a one-man show at Expo, in Montreal.
1969	Serves as photographic adviser to the World Fair held in Osaka, Japan.
1971	*Faces of Our Time* is published. Awarded U.S. Presidential Citation.

1973	Opens a new studio at the Château Laurier.
1983	*Karsh: A Fifty-Year Retrospective* is published.
1987	Beginning of the Karsh collection at the Library and Archives Canada.
1989	Awarded the Gold Medal of the Americas Society for furthering Canadian-American understanding.
1990	Receives the Companion of the Order of Canada.
1992	The studio closes.
1995	Solange Gauthier-Karsh Laboratory opened at the Children's Hospital of Eastern Ontario, Ottawa.
1997	Yousuf and Estrellita move to Boston. Yousuf's camera and equipment are donated to the Canada Science and Technology Museum.
2002, July 13	Yousuf Karsh dies.
2005	Yousuf and Estrellita Karsh Emergency Department is unveiled at the Children's Hospital of Eastern Ontario, Ottawa.

Timeline of Famous Photographs

1933	Prime Minister Robert Borden, Ottawa Little Theatre
1935	Lord and Lady Bessborough
1936	Grey Owl (Archibald Belaney), Prime Minister William Lyon Mackenzie King, President Franklin D. Roosevelt (U.S.A.)
1939	H.R.H. Princess Juliana (Netherlands)
1941	Prime Minister Winston Churchill (U.K.), Paul Robeson (U.S.A)
1943	H.R.H Princess Elizabeth (U.K.), King George VI (U.K.)
1944	Edward Steichen (U.S.A.), Vice President Harry Truman (U.S.A.)
1945	Ibn Abdul Aziz Faisal (later King of Saudi Arabia), Humphrey Bogart (U.S.A.), Elizabeth Taylor (U.S.A.), Portia White
1948	Marian Anderson (U.S.A.), Prime Minister John Costello (Ireland), Helen Keller (U.S.A.), President Herbert Hoover (U.S.A.), The Marx Brothers (U.S.A.)
1949	Prime Minister Clement Attlee (U.K.), Prime Minister Jawaharlal Nehru (India), Pope Pius XII, Jean Sibelius (composer, Finland)
1950	Atlas Steel Company, Prime Minister Liquat Ali Khan (Pakistan)
1951	H.R.H. Princess Elizabeth, Prince Philip, Prince Charles, Princess Anne (U.K.)
1953	Prime Minister Louis St. Laurent
1954	Pablo Casals (Spain), Walt Disney (U.S.A), Pablo Picasso (Spain), Albert Schweitzer (Nobel Peace Prize, France), John Steinbeck (Nobel Prize, literature, U.S.A.)
1955	Prime Minister Harold MacMillan (U.K.), Dag Hammarskjöld (Secretary-General, United Nations, Sweden), Audrey Hepburn (U.S.A.), Georgia O'Keefe (U.S.A.), Norman Rockwell (U.S.A.), President Sukarno (Indonesia)
1957	Glenn Gould, Ernest Hemingway (Nobel Prize, literature, U.S.A.), Senator John F. Kennedy (U.S.A.)
1958	Charles Herbert Best (Nobel Prize, medicine)
1959	President Dwight D. Eisenhower (U.S.A.)
1960	President-elect John F. Kennedy (U.S.A.)
1962	Martin Luther King Jr. (U.S.A.)
1963	President Lyndon Johnson (U.S.A.), Chairman Nikita Khrushchev (U.S.S.R), Prime Minister Harold Wilson (U.K.)
1964	H.R.H. King Constantine (Greece), Prime Minister Alec Douglas Home (U.K.), President Heinrich Luebke (Germany)
1965	Prime Minister Lester Pearson (Nobel Peace Prize), Ossip Zadkine (Paris, Belarus)
1966	President Nasser (Egypt)
1968	Prime Minister Pierre Elliott Trudeau
1969	Apollo XI Crew (Neil Armstrong, Buzz Aldrin, Michael Collins, U.S.A.), Hideki Yukawa (Nobel Prize, physics, Japan)
1970	Muhammad Ali (U.S.A)
1971	President Fidel Castro (Cuba)
1974	Prime Minister John Diefenbaker
1975	H.R.H. Prince Charles (U.K.), Dr. Helen Taussig (U.S.A.)
1977	Margaret Atwood, Robertson Davies, President Gerald Ford (U.S.A), Ansel Adams (U.S.A)

1979	Prime Minister Joseph Clark
	Pope John Paul II
1981	President Jimmy Carter (U.S.A.), President Valéry Giscard d'Estaing (France)
	President François Mitterand (France)
1982	President Ronald Reagan (U.S.A)
1983	President Mohamed Hosni Mubarak (Egypt)
1984	Archbishop Desmond Tutu (Nobel Peace Prize, South Africa)
1985	Prime Minister Brian Mulroney
1988	Wayne Gretzky, Mother Teresa (Nobel Peace Prize)
1989	President Corazon Aquino (Philippines), Prime Minister Benazir Bhutto (Pakistan), Prime Minister Jean Chrétien, President Lech Walesa (Poland)
1990	Robertson Davies, President Mikhail Gorbachev (Russia), President Vaclav Havel (Czechoslovakia), Jim Henson (U.S.A.)
1991	Angela Lansbury, Prime Minister John Major (U.K.)
1992	President Boris Yeltsin (Russia)
1993	President Bill Clinton and Hillary Rodham Clinton (U.S.A.)

Index

Photo by Lou Rioux-Goodall

About the Author

lian goodall has been inventing poems and telling stories since she was two years old. She is the author of four books including *Singing Towards the Future: The Story of Portia White*, which is also in Napoleon Publishing's Stories of Canada series. lian has a kind, patient husband, two wonderful daughters and a lively baby son. She lives north of Toronto, outside the magical village of Kettleby, on a horse farm that is also home to seven black cats, one mischievous dog and is run by a bossy donkey called Omar-Petey. Check her website www.liangoodall.com for news about life at Omar's Jazz Club, lian's new projects and the writing classes she teaches.

Acknowledgements/Resources

The author would like to thank many members of the hard-working staff at:

Bank of Canada, National Currency Collection
Boston Public Library
Canada Science and Technology Museum
Children's Hospital of Eastern Ontario
City of Ottawa Archives
Eastern Townships School Board
Fairmont Château Laurier
George Eastman House, International Museum of Photography and Film
Library and Archives Canada
Muscular Dystrophy Association
Museum of Fine Arts, Boston
Ottawa Little Theatre
Ottawa Public Library
Royal Philatelic Society of Canada
University of Ottawa Library
Parks Canada
Pier 21

The author would like to sincerely thank the people who made the story more meaningful by kindly giving their time through interviews or correspondence, or assisting with materials: Mary Alderman, Jean Comfort, Jerry Fielder, Ernst Frehner, Michael and Ruth Hood, Barbara Karsh, Estrellita Karsh, Salim Karsh, Sid Karsh, Sonja Mortimer, Lesley Pergau and Honourable Raymond Setlakwé. Derek Cooke, Lou Rioux-Goodall and Helen Goodall gave unending and deeply appreciated personal support.

Among those that the author owes special thanks to: Josée Audette, Paul Berry, Debbie Brentnell, David Bullock, Catherine Butler, Rocky Chan, Louise Corriveau, Jill Delaney, Jane Earle, Isabelle Fernandez, Katie Getchel, Anne Havinga, Lynn Lafontaine, Hariette Fried, Anne Grobbo, Sheila O'Hearn, Jean Matheson, Jesse McKee, Members of Canadian Corps of Commissionaires, Mary Munk, Napoleon & Company, Mark Osterman, Robin Riddihough, Aaron Schmidt, Joe R. Struble, Carrie-Anne Smith, Helen P. Graves Smith, Deneen Perrin, Charles J. G. Verge, Margaret Wahl, Fran Ward and Tara Wood.

In addition to consultation of the above sources, Mr. Karsh's thoughts and experiences were brought to light by viewing interviews, reading books and numerous articles by wonderful writers that space does not permit us to mention here. Some of the books Mr. Karsh participated in include: *Canada: as Seen by the Camera of Yousuf Karsh and Described in Words* by John Fisher; *Faces of Destiny; Faces of Our Time; In Search of Greatness: Reflections of Yousuf Karsh; Karsh: American Legends; Karsh: Canadians; Karsh, a Fifty-Year Retrospective; Karsh: A Sixty-Year Retrospective; Karsh Portfolio; Portraits of Greatness; These are the Sacraments; This is the Mass; This is Rome: a Pilgrimage in Words and Pictures; Yousuf Karsh: Heroes of Light and Shadow.*

Photo and Art Credits